Praise for
Leading with a Limp
by Dan B. Allender, PhD

"There are good books on leadership, but this one is profound. It is better than a 'how to do it' book; this is a 'how to *be* it' book for leaders. Dan Allender offers serious wisdom rather than simple platitudes."

—MARK SANBORN, speaker, leadership consultant, and best-selling
author of *The Fred Factor*

"Not only is Dan Allender a good friend, he is a great leader. In *Leading with a Limp*, he has shown us how we can effectively lead those allotted to our charge. Read this book; it will bring a lot of things into perspective for you."

—DENNIS RAINEY, president of FamilyLife and coauthor
of *Moments Together for Couples*

"After I read this book, the first two words out of my mouth were 'At last!' Amid a deluge of spiritual gifts' inventories, at last there is someone who understands how God's strength is made *perfect* in our imperfections. At last someone has brought spiritual strengths and spiritual weaknesses into conversation. For Dan Allender, the limp is a limpid way of walking that leads into the very presence of God."

—LEONARD SWEET, author of *The Three Hardest Words*
and *Out of the Question...Into the Mystery*

"*Leading with a Limp* is not your basic cafeteria-brand manual on how to do leadership. It is a call to openly face your shortcomings as a leader. Dan Allender reminds us that our greatest asset as leaders is not our competence but th⟨...⟩ ⟨...⟩ to name and deal with our frailties and imperfections."

—DR. CRAWFORD W. LORITTS JR., author, speaker
of Fellowship Bible Church in Roswell, Georgia

"Once again Dan Allender has propelled us headlong into the paradoxical wonders of the gospel of God's grace. *Leading with a Limp* exposes the thin veneer of respectability we leaders try to stretch over our destructive idols of control and pragmatism. In so doing, Allender invites us to the freeing humility of leading as "the chief sinner" in whatever context God has placed us."

—SCOTTY SMITH, founding pastor of Christ Community Church
in Franklin, Tennessee, and coauthor of *Restoring Broken Things*

"I often wonder if other people feel the way I do when they read books on leadership. Most of the books are heavy on motivation or strategy or positive thinking. Dan Allender looks at how anyone can move his team—and himself—forward when he is pummeled by circumstances and his heart is fainting. This is real-world stuff, but you'll have to take off the rose-colored glasses to read it."

—BOB LEPINE, cohost of FamilyLife Today

"*Leading with a Limp* will have a lasting impact on me; it addressed several issues I'm struggling with at this point in my life and leadership. I thank God for this honest and insightful book!"

—BRIAN MCLAREN, pastor and author of *The Secret Message of Jesus*
and *A New Kind of Christian*

LEADING
WITH A LIMP

WORKBOOK

LEADING
WITH A LIMP

DISCOVER HOW TO TURN YOUR STRUGGLES INTO STRENGTHS

DAN B. ALLENDER, PhD
AND MATTHEW D. BAUGHER

WATERBROOK
PRESS

LEADING WITH A LIMP WORKBOOK
PUBLISHED BY WATERBROOK PRESS
12265 Oracle Boulevard, Suite 200
Colorado Springs, Colorado 80921
A division of Random House Inc.

ISBN 1-57856-953-2

Printed in the United States of America
2006—First Edition

10 9 8 7 6 5 4 3 2 1

CONTENTS

THE DAILY PRACTICE
OF LIMPING LEADERSHIP

Since you picked up this workbook, we're assuming you have read at least part of the companion book *Leading with a Limp*. If so, you arrive at this page either convinced or confused by the following truths about leaders who limp. As a leader, you are:

- powerful and powerless
- incredibly influential but seemingly lacking in impact
- energized but weary
- clear about your vision but also confused
- impassioned but reluctant
- successful but often feeling like a failure
- called to be a prophet, a priest, and a king

These are just a few of the paradoxes of leadership, and they are as real as your ability to live within the tension they create. This workbook is designed to help you implement in practical ways the concepts and principles of limping leadership—in the face of these tensions.

If you are a pastor or a CEO, a teacher or a committee chair, a parent or a youth worker—if there is any person who looks to you for help, for direction, or for vision—

you're a leader. And because leadership is such a multifaceted subject, we'll concentrate on a few essential areas. As you read the stories and answer the questions in the chapters that follow, you will:

- Identify your natural leadership tendencies and assess how your routines, habits, and personality traits influence—both positively and negatively—your effectiveness as a leader.
- Examine your character in light of God's character, because it is essential that leaders not only have character but also bring their unique character to bear in leadership.
- Consider the stories of others who exhibit the power of broken leadership.
- Take practical steps toward maturing as a leader by confessing that you are your organization's "chief sinner" and then using your flaws to lead with power and effectiveness.

WHAT ARE YOU FOLLOWING?

Leaders are people who have followers. Likewise, all leaders follow someone or something. Robert K. Greenleaf, in his book *The Power of Servant Leadership,* says this: "It is just as important to be discriminating in choosing whom to follow as it is to prepare to lead."[1]

Who and what you follow largely determines both your approach to leadership and the expectations you place on yourself as a leader. Without thinking too long or too hard about your answer, write in the space that follows—in no more than two sentences—your philosophy of leadership.

Now read what you've written and ask yourself, *What is the source of my leadership philosophy?* Does your philosophy have to do with increasing profits and market share, beating the competition, introducing new products and services, or increasing value for shareholders? If you lead in the context of a church or ministry, does your philosophy have to do with increasing attendance, creating a larger donor base, generating new ministries, or extending the reach of your ministry? Or do you see yet another model reflected in the words you wrote?

Now read your philosophy of leadership one more time and notice how close it comes to describing your daily actions as a leader. Does it reflect who you *really are* as a leader or who you think you *should* be? As you lead others, who and what are you *really* following?

Every leader has to operate in the presence of five constant leadership challenges: crisis, complexity, betrayal, loneliness, and weariness. If you have served in positions of leadership for any length of time, you are already familiar with each of these. However, you may not have accepted the fact that they are always present and always in collusion with one another. A primary advantage and core strength of limping leadership is that it enables you to recognize and understand the five challenges of leadership—and to use them to enhance your effectiveness. *7-17-06*

Being Led by the Least of These

Few metaphors are so representative of an aspect of life that they transform the way we think about ourselves. But such is the power of the following story about a boy who died too young in Bombay, India. Santoosh spent his life in a filthy slum and died an orphan. His brief and tragic existence, however, teaches us much of what we need to know about limping leadership.

Before he was seven years old, Santoosh lost both his parents to AIDS. Whenever he chanced to see his reflection, a thinning face would stare back at him. In one of his final moments, he was visited by Christian speaker and singer Kathy Troccoli, members of a mission team from Life Outreach International, and me (Matt).

Now, an interesting thing happens when you tour an Indian slum: you notice how many people are smiling. The children are running around, laughing, and doing the things that kids do. It doesn't seem to matter to them that a foul stench hangs in the air or that rats are running along with them as they search for their next "treasure" among the heaps of trash. Most of the kids want to introduce themselves to me, the stranger, and find out my name.

We take a right turn and then a left. After another right we find ourselves in a narrow maze of concrete alleys. Each small passageway has a five-inch-wide river flowing down the middle, providing a rudimentary sewage system. No protection here other than watching where I step. Faces, each one telling a lifetime of stories in only a matter of seconds, peek out of openings that must be doors and windows. The faces are filled with curiosity, and they smile broadly when smiled upon.

A man walking behind me has found a young child, perhaps two years old, who is absolutely giddy as he is suspended over the man's head. The child's eyes speak for him: "Again! Again!" The man obliges. Amid the laughter behind us, we begin to look closer at our surroundings and discover the other constant of the Indian slum—great suffering. "Santoosh is just ahead," our guide tells us.

We finally arrive at Santoosh's room. It is dark and hot. On a concrete shelf just inside the door rests an old toothbrush, its very angle on the stoop representing its honored place in the household. To the left sits a pot with something inside that is either food or refuse. Even after I glance a second time, the answer eludes me. The boy's grandmother welcomes us, and we meet Santoosh. He is seated on a bed directly in front of us, and it is no exaggeration to say he possesses one of the sweetest and purest faces I have ever had the pleasure of seeing. But his health is obviously not good. His body looks like that of a four-year-old, not the seven-year-old who actually inhabits the skeletal frame. Kathy takes a seat to his left and immediately says, "Oh, he's burning up! He's so hot!" She gently wraps her arm around his shoulders and cups her hand under his chin. He melts into the embrace of her touch. Our interpreter is speaking to the grandmother and learning all about the last couple of years. Santoosh listens in a way that shows he is resigned to the harsh reality of his plight.

Eventually, Santoosh speaks the word *papa*. He points over Kathy's shoulder. "Papa," he repeats. On a shelf above the bed sits a picture in a beat-up frame. It shows a man with a mustache, and it has the off-color glow of a photo from *Life* magazine twenty-five years ago. Or, in this case, the faded look of something that has suffered too much exposure to the sun and the elements.

"Is this your papa?"

The boy nods.

We capture some of this moment on video to help others understand the great need in India. Kathy holds the photo of Santoosh's father, turns to the camera, and begins to explain the situation. As she speaks, Santoosh reaches to the photo in her lap and begins to stroke it. He appears to be both loving his father and sweeping the dust off the glass. His malnourished hand then reaches down and brushes some dust off Kathy's leg. She would later say that she had never experienced Christ as she did when that hand touched her. The Bible makes it clear that Jesus is found among the young, the poor, and the suffering—among "the least of these" (Matthew 25:45). Jesus was as real in that room as the concrete wall I leaned against.

The missions team was able to get Santoosh to a doctor, and he began to receive long-overdue medical help. We left Bombay with a sense that he was going to improve. But Santoosh died just three months later in a hospital in Bandra, the same day I wrote this story. In his short life he had suffered too many trials from which his body simply could not recover.

A young boy named Santoosh, sick and poverty stricken in a Bombay slum, was a more powerful leader than most adults I have known. That's because leadership doesn't come only from the head; it comes from the heart as well. So the next time you send out a memo on how to improve your organization's performance, make sure your people already know your heart. It's the head that understands, but the heart that follows.

The story of Santoosh and his short life helped Life Outreach International raise more than a half-million dollars to open a center outside Bombay. The facility will house one hundred and fifty children. Besides feeding and clothing them, it will also teach them how to read and how to have a relationship with God. The footage of Kathy Troccoli's tears continues to make very real a situation from which many of us try to distance ourselves.

Imagine if our group had instead interviewed a ranking government official. He would have explained the plight of millions of children in his country. He would have used graphs, statistics, and maybe even photos. The story of poverty and suffering can be communicated with both approaches. But in this instance, which leader has more power and influence—a dying seven-year-old boy or an educated, articulate, and well-trained government official?

FOLLOWING A LEADER

I'd much rather follow the leader whose life compels tears. When Kathy was meeting the next day with abandoned children at a crowded train station, she became so overwhelmed that she asked the cameras to stop so she could have a break. Upon seeing her tears, a young boy asked the interpreter, "Why is she crying?"

"She's crying for you."

"Really?"

Within minutes the boy was offering half his food to Kathy.

That is undeniable leadership. It's powerful, effective, and authentic. Stop for a moment and consider Santoosh's story in light of the constant pitfalls that every leader confronts:

- *Crisis:* For Santoosh the daily crisis was meager resources and a frail body.
- *Complexity:* Santoosh had much to teach the rest of the world, but no way to get his message out.
- *Betrayal:* The young boy's body was betrayed by sickness and malnutrition. His government was no help, and his parents had died.
- *Loneliness:* He had no one left but his grandmother, and she was powerless to do anything.
- *Weariness:* In the end he was too weak and feverish to even leave his room.

Yet during our visit to Bombay, Kathy Troccoli was empowered by Santoosh's leadership, and she used that power to lead others. Kathy had to confront the same leadership pitfalls that faced Santoosh:

- *Crisis:* The need of India's children is overwhelming.

- *Complexity:* The challenge, without appearing manipulative, is to reach willing hearts: people who will lead others to address the needs.
- *Betrayal:* The twin forces of greed and apathy conspire to keep millions of children mired in poverty and disease.
- *Loneliness:* God is present, yet in our humanness we wonder why he seems to hide—and to do so little to alleviate suffering.
- *Weariness:* Kathy is just one woman trying to generate help for an overwhelming number of suffering children.

YOUR LIFE AS A LEADER

Choose an example from your life as a leader. (You probably need look no further than something that happened this week.) Using the five challenges of leadership as a lens through which to look at that situation, identify the biggest leadership pitfalls confronting you right now. Write down the specifics under the appropriate headings to follow.

Crisis

Complexity

Betrayal

Loneliness

Weariness

HOW TO GET THE MOST FROM THIS WORKBOOK

The *Leading with a Limp Workbook* is designed to help you mature as a leader by making the most of your brokenness. The image of the limping leader is found throughout Scripture. Jacob wrestled all night with God, and in the morning he still would not let go. He walked away from that episode with a permanent limp and with a new name—Israel (see Genesis 32:24–31). Moses, a murderer and one of history's most reluctant leaders, emancipated an entire nation. Paul, who made it clear that he was a greater sinner than any other person on earth, took the gospel to the Gentiles and wrote much of the New Testament (see 1 Timothy 1:15–16). He also described a permanent "limp" that he received from God, but he knew from daily experience that he gained strength in weakness (see 2 Corinthians 12:7–10).

Our purpose in writing this workbook is to help you view leadership in a completely different light—to see it in the inverted way that Jesus taught and modeled. In other words, to gain your life, you must first lose your life; to prevail, you must draw from the power of brokenness; to enlist followers, you must be honest about your weaknesses and your failures; to lead effectively and with power, you must lead with a limp.

The stories, questions, and exercises in this workbook are designed to help you explore in greater depth the ideas presented in the book *Leading with a Limp*. This workbook will help you assess and rethink your approach to leadership. Let it be a guide into the deeper regions of your life as a leader.

As you answer the questions in the chapters that follow, don't worry about coming up with the "right" answer. The point is to look honestly at your life, your heart, and your practice of leading others. If the number of questions feels daunting, answer in short phrases or feel free to jump ahead to a question that applies more directly to your experience as a leader.

IDEAS FOR GROUP USE

Although the questions in this workbook are designed to be first answered individually, this guide also has great value when used as a group study and discussion guide. It will prove to be a valuable resource for team building, leadership development, accountability groups, ministry training, and small groups interested in the topic of leadership.

If you do this study with a group, remember that talking candidly about struggles and challenges in leadership can be threatening. So have the group agree to the following ground rules:

- *Listen well.* Don't interrupt the person who is speaking. Instead of thinking about what you plan to say next, consider what the stories of other group members reveal about leadership and its challenges.
- *Maintain confidentiality.* If your group is not a safe place for people to talk about the hard issues surrounding leadership, it will fail to fully serve its purpose. Agree in advance that nothing that is said will be repeated outside the group.
- *Encourage depth.* Take the risk of telling candid, authentic stories about both the difficulties and the joys of leadership. Each group member will get more from the group experience if openness is the rule of the day.

1

The Best Leaders Are Reluctant

Confession is never easy, but it can be instructive. Take a moment to reread the opening story in chapter 1 of *Leading with a Limp*. Surely I (Dan) am not alone in my experiences. The names and context will be different for every leader who reads my confession, but most of us have been in similar situations. Think about which story you would tell if you were sharing your own leadership confession with trusted friends or colleagues.

Does your story reflect some reluctance? I'm guessing so—but isn't it good to know that even the best leaders are reluctant? For prime examples, we need look no further than Moses or the apostle Paul. No matter how confident a leader appears on the outside, no matter how bold he is in his decision making, no matter how dazzling his vision for the organization or ministry, if you could look into the soul of some of the leaders you admire most, you would find a person who is reluctant to do precisely what he has been called to do. And it's a good thing this is true.

When we consider the top requirements for a leader—whether in the church, corporate America, or government—we should check to see if that person has first done her best to escape leadership and then has been compelled to return to put her hand to the tiller. This was the most common path for God's leaders in the Bible. God loves reluctant leaders, and a big reason for this is that they are not easily seduced by power, pride, or ambition.

POWER

A reluctant leader is highly suspicious of people who work to accumulate power. In fact, one of the reasons godly leaders are reluctant is that they have seen power wrongly used to build personal kingdoms rather than to lead. Reluctant leaders not only don't aspire to hold power, they work to give it away. The reluctant leader detoxifies power by empowering others to bring their vision, passion, and gifts to the enterprise. He creates an environment of open debate that honors differences of viewpoint but generates no fear of reprisal.

1. Describe a time when, as a leader, you struggled with power. Were you seeking more power, misusing the power you had, or being victimized by someone else's use and abuse of power? Explain.

2. What has been the long-range impact of this experience? What effect did it have on the way you view power and the way you use your power in leadership?

PRIDE

A reluctant leader is not likely to be trapped in the limelight of pride. Remember, she is the one who fled from leadership, not the one who schemed to gain the top position. No reluctant leader is impressed with her own ability, because she knows that her intelligence, skill, talent, and ability are all gifts from God. Besides, as Paul wrote, God didn't choose the wise or the strong, but the weak and the foolish (see 1 Corinthians 1:27).

3. Think back to a time when, in your role as a leader, you struggled with pride. What prompted that struggle? Through what action, speech, and/or attitude did your pride make itself known? What happened to make you aware that it was, in fact, a manifestation of pride?

4. What has been the long-term impact of this experience? What effect did it have on the way you view yourself and your role as a leader?

AMBITION

The ambitious leader relentlessly pushes to do more, to build a bigger church or organization, to attract more notice. Enough is never enough—no matter the cost to people or the process. The ends justify the means.

Not so with the reluctant leader. He is not looking for status or a larger office, nor does he invest in the makings of a personal kingdom. Instead, he wants to see others exceed their greatest dreams. Every good teacher wants his students to take their work further than he was able to do. To be exceeded is the dream of a reluctant leader. To be replaced is the goal, not at all a sign of failure.

5. Recall a time when you struggled with ambition. What impact did it have on your effectiveness as a leader? What effect did it have on your organization?

6. What has been the long-range impact of this experience? What effect has your struggle with ambition had on the way you view yourself? on the way you view your role as a leader?

7. Looking back at the circumstances now with the clarity that hindsight offers, why were you able to deceive yourself about your ambition? What made you think it was something else, something that honored God?

A Reluctant Leader in Action

Being a reluctant leader is not second best; it is the pattern we see in the Bible. Scripture and secular history record reluctant leaders enjoying great success and performing legendary accomplishments. Other reluctant leaders are battered by the frustration and, as a result, self-doubt of leadership and discover a deeper meaning. My friend Rick falls into the latter category. In the past year he has shown me (Matt) the power and force of authentic humility at work in his life as a leader.

Rick is a psychiatrist who revels in and celebrates the chaos of life. He has been the reluctant teacher of an adult Sunday-school class at my church for the past eleven years, and during the week he is a researcher at Vanderbilt University. His life involves going back and forth between professional therapy, statistical research, and the constant demands of soliciting new grant money. For anyone who has never had to engage the machinery of applying for federal grants, let me just say it's not for the faint of heart.

Rick has a way of disarming you with his vulnerability and his various idiosyncrasies. He's one of those guys who, although he's a very calm speaker, gets so much energy going through his body that he almost loses his breath. And attending his Sunday-school class is like going to your own private therapy session. The class tends to get off on some beautiful but time-consuming tangents. I think Rick sees every detour as a great adventure. His approach to life is described perfectly by G. K. Chesterton: "An adventure is only an inconvenience rightly considered. An inconvenience is only an adventure wrongly considered."[1]

Every week Rick comes in with pages of notes and a full outline for that week's class. He usually gets through the first paragraph. And this is what is so endearing: the following week he'll come in with another stack of pages only to barely touch them. I'd sure like to see what jewels lie buried in all those years' worth of unused notes.

One topic that Rick, age fifty-one, loves to talk about is the supernatural change that has taken place in his life. He has told us at various times and in different ways about finally learning to rest in the love and sovereignty of God. He's a walking paradox of honesty. It is so obvious that he, like the rest of us, struggles with spiritual issues on a daily basis. But it's impossible *not* to catch a glimpse of the transformation that God has worked in his life. I have never heard him mention the love of God when he hasn't gotten a catch in his throat or a tear in his eye. It's a Pavlovian response of the purest kind; it's caused by the work of our redeeming God.

On a recent Sunday we were discussing the day's sermon, which dealt with the four stages of growth in faith: moral apathy, moral concern, moral despair, and holy delight. Some individuals go through these stages sequentially, and in those instances the stages unfold over a lifetime. More often, though, we tend to bounce around in an unpredictable pattern, but Rick maintains that we won't ever truly grow until we spend some time in moral despair. It's a very difficult thing to jump directly from moral concern to holy delight. Why is that? Because to recognize God's magnificent gift of grace, we must first come to terms with our moral depravity. The genuine recognition of our sinfulness has to be personal for each one of us.

Maybe that is one reason God seeks out reluctant leaders. Until we can accept the truth that we are the chief sinner in our organization, the effectiveness of our work as leaders will be stunted.

8. What about yourself comes to mind when you read the apostle Paul's confession: "Christ Jesus came into the world to save sinners—of whom I am the worst. But for that very reason I was shown mercy so that in me, the worst of sinners, Christ Jesus might display his unlimited patience as an example for those who would believe on him and receive eternal life" (1 Timothy 1:15–16)? In what ways was Paul the world's biggest sinner? What does his statement suggest about your own ranking among sinners?

9. Do you think Paul was using hyperbole to make a point? Why or why not? (Keep in mind that he was guilty of conspiracy to imprison and kill innocent people simply because they had embraced faith in the Jewish Messiah.)

10. In your work as a leader, what "chief sinner" experience have you had recently? Describe it here.

Rick is familiar with the experience of being the chief sinner. He is also open about how long it has taken him to reach the point of moral despair, which leads to humble dependence on Christ. Rick acknowledges that he is still as messed up and as confused as he's ever been, but now he has experienced the holy delight of pure communion with his Creator.

Last week, however, a member of the class had a revelation. "Wait a minute, Rick. I've been coming to this class for eleven years. Are you telling me that you've just now started to figure all this out, that you didn't really believe it before?"

That is a difficult question to answer. Put yourself in Rick's position. He's the leader. He's been teaching a class of adults almost every Sunday for more than a decade. Is he really saying that he is just now getting it?

Rick simply said, "Amazing, isn't it?"

He might be a reluctant teacher of this adult Sunday-school class, but as a leader he gets it. And he is changing our lives by allowing us to watch God change his. That's a leader. How do I know that? Because there are doctors, lawyers, musicians, grocery-store workers, bus drivers, and homemakers in that class, and they would follow Rick anywhere. He leads the class members with a discernible limp, but I wouldn't dream of criticizing that limp. I only pray that God gives me one that's half as noticeable.

The Advantages of Being Reluctant

Most followers assume that the best leaders are those who have confidence to spare. But if you look at the leaders God commissioned, you'll find men and women who were so reluctant to lead that in some instances they worked hard to talk God out of calling them. After all, if you have even the slightest inkling of the hard realities of leadership, you would never willingly submit yourself to the role. Reluctance is actually the only sane way to enter the work of leadership. And the paradox is that reluctance brings major benefits. Reluctance makes leaders more courageous, more deeply creative, more grateful, more open to others, and more hopeful.

Reluctant Leaders Are More Courageous

Being a leader involves facing crises—and that is only one of the aspects of leadership that gives rise to fear. No leader escapes crises, but you can't allow fear to be your guide. As my friend Rick says, "If you don't believe that you operate out of fear, see me after class and I'll prove to you that you do!"

11. Think about some of the fears you experience as a leader. Now focus on an experience in which you had the courage to lead even though your natural tendency would have been to hide or place blame. Tell that story briefly in the space below.

12. In the situation you just described, what enabled you to lead with courage rather than be defeated by fear?

Reluctant Leaders Go Deeper to Find Creative Solutions

The world of leadership is so complex that no one can fully impose order on the chaos. Leaders know that hardly anything works and that, if something does work, it never works well or for very long. Regular recalibration is inevitable, and it forces us to dig deeper for new alternatives, making us more creative.

I (Matt) have been guiding people in their careers for almost twenty years, and this much I know: the good days are never as good as they seem, and the bad days are never as bad as they seem. We leaders know intrinsically that positive or negative circumstances are temporary. We also know that change is constant. To transform a negative process into a positive one, we must resist the tendency to narrow our options and instead creatively broaden the range of possible solutions.

13. Think about the most recent great day you experienced as a leader. What happened after that day to bring you back to the normal setting? What type of complexity did that shift back to normal introduce into your work as a leader?

14. Now think about the last terrible day you experienced. How terrible was it, really, when you woke up the next morning? What happened to lessen the effects of that terrible day?

15. What did you do to tap into your creativity and to broaden your options in addressing change and complexity?

Reluctant Leaders Are More Grateful

As you lead others, you realize that no leadership can happen without relationship. And as you grow in leadership, you will reach a place of being grateful for those around you, even those who are difficult and impossible to understand. Leaders know the pain of betrayal from enemies and friends alike. But we can learn to be grateful even for the betrayals because such assaults teach us something unique. Effective leaders also learn from both praise and criticism—even when they are undeserved.

16. List the people in your organization for whom you are grateful. Take time to thank God for each person by name.

17. Next, list the people for whom you *need* to be grateful. Note instances of betrayal linked to anyone on this list. Now take a few minutes to think about a lesson you learned as a result of that betrayal, a lesson that you could not have learned any other way. Thank God for using the pain of betrayal to teach you and shape you into the leader he wants you to be.

Reluctant Leaders Are More Open to Others

Leadership is isolating. Some people in your organization want your position, so they will oppose you no matter what you do. Others will support you until you make a hard decision that runs counter to what they wanted to happen. It's lonely at the top, but a reluctant leader remains open to others no matter how much opposition she faces.

Limping leaders don't waste energy developing scenarios designed purely for self-defense or self-justification. Instead, they move forward with their plan of action and invite everyone in the organization to join them.

Consider the example set by the apostle Paul, a prisoner being transported by ship to Rome. Here is how Luke described the scene after Paul and his traveling companions were shipwrecked on Malta following a horrific storm:

> As Paul gathered an armful of sticks and was laying them on the fire, a poisonous snake, driven out by the heat, fastened itself onto his hand. The people of the island saw it hanging there and said to each other, "A murderer, no doubt! Though he escaped the sea, justice will not permit him to live." But Paul shook off the snake into the fire and was unharmed. The people

waited for him to swell up or suddenly drop dead. But when they had waited a long time and saw no harm come to him, they changed their minds. (Acts 28:3–6, NLT)

After the snake bit Paul, he didn't feel compelled to defend his reputation against the crowd's false assumptions. He didn't immediately say, "I know what your customs tell you, but you have to trust that I am no murderer!" Instead, Paul went on about his business. And when the islanders saw no harm come to him, they changed their minds. So stay the course, remain open to everyone—both allies and antagonists—and you will outlast your opposition.

18. List the people in your organization who most often oppose you. Have you wasted energy in self-defense while trying to prove them wrong? Try to recall an instance in which your self-defense won over an opponent. It is most likely a very difficult task.

19. Think about the primary reasons you feel lonely as a leader. Identify any times when you have closed yourself off from others and deepened your own loneliness? What can you do to stay open to everyone—your allies and your antagonists alike? Be specific.

Reluctant Leaders Are More Hopeful

Leadership is wrought with pressure, demands, and frustration. The call to leadership demands everything you have and then some, and the constant challenge is how to hold onto hope in spite of your weariness.

One way to cultivate that hope is, as a reluctant leader, to help others achieve their potential and exceed their greatest dreams. Leading in a way that promotes justice, combats evil, and works to secure the good brings the greatest joy in leadership. Still, the work is exhausting. So meditate on this word of encouragement from the apostle Paul:

> Let us not become weary in doing good, for at the proper time we will reap a
> harvest if we do not give up. (Galatians 6:9)

Don't give in to discouragement. Don't let the weariness of leadership steal your hope. Instead, find joy in serving those you lead and trust that God will open your eyes to the good that you are doing.

20. Think back to a time when your work as a leader advanced what is good and diminished what is evil. Briefly describe the circumstances and the outcome.

21. Think back to the last leader, teacher, or mentor who expressed deep joy
    when he or she saw you succeed. What emotions did that person's joy elicit
    in you? What happened to your motivation? Now think of one way you can
    help people in your organization realize their potential in some aspect of
    their work or ministry. Choose one person to start with and make plans
    to begin that effort this week.

Those who ran from leadership and were later cornered by God to serve as leaders saw their service expose their weakness and reveal God's goodness. So, yes, the best
leaders are reluctant. But are they fulfilled? Absolutely.

2

COUNTING THE COST
OF YOUR CALLING

In your work as a leader, you can probably identify closely with some of these statements from chapter 2 of *Leading with a Limp:*

- We have adversaries who want not merely to replace us but to destroy us.
- With the best wisdom available and much reflection and prayer, leaders decide. And often the decision sets into motion the next crisis.
- If you lead, you will eventually serve with Judas or Peter.
- The leader is often the only one tossing and turning all night over his decisions and the consequences of his decisions, both of which lead to personal criticism.

Realizing that all leaders deal with such challenges tells you that you are not alone in the struggles you experience. The good news is that the pitfalls of leadership can be motivating opportunities, not paralyzing obstacles.

THE FIVE CHALLENGES OF LEADERSHIP

If you weren't convinced that God called you into leadership, you might find a good place to hide—and you'd stay there. But God knew what he was doing when he called you to lead others in the face of crisis, complexity, betrayal, loneliness, and weariness—the five constant challenges of leadership.

In light of these contrasts, it's essential that you count the cost of God's calling. As you answer the following questions related to the five challenges of leadership, use the charts on pages 8 and 9 in the introduction to *Leading with a Limp* to help you think about both your default responses to these five challenges and the most effective response to each challenge.

Crisis

Leading is all about moving toward a goal while confronting significant obstacles with limited resources in the midst of uncertainty and with people who may or may not come through in a pinch. There is no way to plan for all the contingencies or have all the knowledge we need. Crisis is a context for opportunity and growth, but it also reminds us that we are fundamentally not in control. We are dependent on God's grace, on a host of people and circumstances that operate well beyond our control, and on the perspiration we have expended in anticipation of the unknown. As leaders, we live on the edge of disaster every day.

1. Identify the crisis that is currently testing you. What about this particular crisis is pushing you to the edge? Be specific.

2. What is your typical response to crisis—hiding, trying to control, blaming, working harder, or something else? Does your default response usually help you cope with crisis, or does it hinder your ability to lead your organization through the crisis?

3. What would you like to do in response to a crisis?

Complexity

All leaders deal with competing values, demands, priorities, and perspectives. Behind the scenes of any church, ministry, or business lies a succession of impossible decisions that go far beyond developing a mission statement or achieving operational goals. Always the bigger question lingers: what is the right thing to do?

As the leader you make decisions that increasingly feel like choosing where the ball is going to land on a roulette wheel. You make the best decision possible given limited data and your own human frailties, and even the best decision might lead to greater complexity.

4. Identify the most complex matter currently confronting you and your organization. What about this issue, choice, or circumstance makes it difficult for you to determine the right decision or course of action?

5. What's your typical response to complexity? Does your default response guide you well, or does it impede your ability to effectively deal with complexity?

6. What would you like to do in response to complexity?

Betrayal

If you lead, you will be betrayed. Jesus was the only leader who never made a mistake, yet he endured the betrayal of both enemy and intimate friend. No matter who betrays you, the wound goes deep. David described it with these words:

If an enemy were insulting me,
> I could endure it;
if a foe were raising himself against me,
> I could hide from him.
But it is you, a man like myself,
> my companion, my close friend,
with whom I once enjoyed sweet fellowship
> as we walked with the throng at the house of God. (Psalm 55:12–14)

It is nearly impossible for a betrayed leader to escape both self-doubt and self-recrimination: *Why didn't I see it coming? Am I as bad as this person says?* Part of the helplessness experienced by a betrayed leader is the inability to set the record straight. It's no wonder that betrayal lies at the root of many of our biggest leadership crises.

7. Describe your most recent experience with being betrayed. Who betrayed you, and was that person a friend, colleague, competitor, or enemy?

8. What is your typical response to betrayal? Does your default response vary according to the relationship you have with the betrayer?

9. What do you do with the hurt that comes with being betrayed by a friend or colleague?

10. What would you like to do in response to the betrayal?

Loneliness

The loneliness that leaders experience is far more than just being alone. It is the awareness that we are set apart for a task and a calling that often deprive us of normal social ties and interaction. In addition, leaders are called to make hard decisions and choices that are guaranteed to disappoint someone—if not many. And that disappointment usually leads to negative reactions and to consequences that the leader must face alone. Loneliness in leadership is isolating and inevitable.

11. What is the most acute loneliness you experience as a leader? What are the causes of that loneliness? What about your work as a leader tends to reduce the number of close friendships?

12. What is your typical response to the loneliness of leadership? Does your default response enhance your connection to others, or does it contribute to deeper loneliness?

13. What would you like to do to address this loneliness?

Weariness

Few leaders, no matter what boundaries they enforce and what margins they build into their lives, can glide through their labor unaffected. Caring for others takes everything we have. But our weariness is not so much about being drained by such stress. It involves our core struggle to hold on to hope. Exhaustion tempts us to despair when we need to press forward in the conviction that unseen glory awaits us (see Galatians 6:9–10).

14. Name the primary causes of weariness in your work as a leader. What demand or energy drain most often pushes you to the point of giving up?

15. What is your typical response to circumstances that tempt you to lose hope?

16. What would you like to do in response when you are in the grip of weariness and on the verge of despair?

What to Do About Fear

Leadership requires character, maturity, and trust. The call to lead others forces you into risk and uncertainty. And no matter how talented and confident you are, there isn't a leader alive who does not deal with fear. The fear of failure is one of the most common, but any of the leadership challenges can give rise to fear that can immobilize you.

As you think about the problem of fear, consider what Alan Downs writes in his book *The Fearless Executive:*

Fear lives only in the mind. At first glance, this may seem painfully obvious, but take a minute to seriously consider the fact that fear does not exist in your environment—it lives solely in your mind. Fear is something that you do to yourself. No one can make you afraid except you.[1]

When our actions and decisions are prompted by fear, we often treat that fear as if it were a tangible enemy present in external circumstances: "I am afraid because X-Y-Z is happening." We convince ourselves that fear is the only rational reaction to the situation when in fact fear is mostly irrational.

17. Do you agree with the statement that fear is *not* caused by external circumstances but is a product of your own response to your circumstances? Explain.

18. If fear is a function of what is going on inside you, what external circumstances and primary leadership challenges elicit that fearful response? List five examples.

19. Look at the list you just made and identify the specific element that prompts fear. For example, if you happened to put down *deadlines,* the specific element might be *no time to think and check my work.*

One of my clients gave me (Matt) a pewter paperweight. It sits on a table near my phone so that I see it often. A question is engraved on its face: "What would you attempt to do if you knew you could not fail?" Thinking about my answer to that question takes me somewhere in my mind as well as my heart. The same question can be asked somewhat differently: "What would you attempt to do if you truly believed that failure was a gift from God as sure and as good as success?"

Limping leaders know that many of their weaknesses arise out of their fears, and one of the greatest fears is the fear of failure. Key to overcoming that fear is to keep moving forward no matter what the outcome may be. If that outcome makes us stronger instead of more bitter, it is not a failure but a victory.

Granted, at times we must sit back and listen for God to speak to us. Most times, however, we pray on the run. We make decisions in the blink of an eye, and with every decision we also choose whether to build an exit door or keep leading. When we step back and look at the bigger picture, we begin to see God's hand at work. It helps us ignore the temptation of exit doors and prompts us to keep moving. We move…God leads. God moves…we follow.

Wherever that following takes you, remember that God has authored the leadership position you are in. Should you succeed, you have the privilege of praising God for his grace and thanking him for the opportunity to serve others. Should you fail, you can praise God for his grace and thank him for the opportunity to serve others. The outcome doesn't matter all that much. Your worth and purpose are not based on any temporal measure of success. God doesn't love you or provide for you according to what your title is, how much you're paid, whether you are the object of adulation or criticism. In all circumstances God is the Author, and you can thank him and praise him for any outcome.

But God can't guide you if you're not moving. So let's get moving.

A CASE STUDY IN FAILED LEADERSHIP

As you read the first part of chapter 3 in *Leading with a Limp,* did you think the Isakson Construction Company was a real corporation, or were you onto me (Dan) by the second page? In deciding to tell the story of Jacob as a case study of a family business, I wanted to show that the Bible has more to teach us on leadership than we sometimes realize. Johan Isakson (Isaac), founder and CEO of an incredibly successful construction company, saw his corporation produce profits as well as jealousy, greed, and contempt within his family.

Johan's sons, Jake (Jacob) and Herman (Esau), as well as his wife, Becky (Rebecca), all attempt to steer the succession of leadership in their favor. Fortunately for Jake/Jacob, God eventually puts him in a situation where he learns how to become a limping leader. In fact, Jacob is the Bible's poster child for limping leadership. He begins life as Jacob (meaning "deceiver"), and he shrewdly works all the angles in his own favor. But after wrestling all night with God, he walks away with a limp and a new name, Israel, which later becomes the name of the nation of God's people. Jacob received a glorious name, but his life is far from a success story.

In the unfolding of the case study of Isakson Construction Company, the following statement is made in chapter 3 of *Leading with a Limp:* "[Jacob] has been set up by the shrewdest player of all: God." Does God really set us up to fail? And is failure the core lesson of limping leadership, a lesson with benefits that God doesn't want us to miss out on?

20. Limping leaders learn that their weakness is not a liability but rather the path to effectiveness. We see examples of this in the Old Testament (Joseph, Moses, Jonah, Jacob, Esther, and many others) as well as in the New Testament (Peter, Paul, John Mark). Do you agree that God *still* prefers to work through limping leaders today? Explain.

21. Limping leaders know that failure is neither fatal nor final. Moses didn't free the Hebrews from Pharaoh's iron grip with his first request of the ruler—or even with the first plague. In fact, the book of Exodus shows that God worked behind the scenes to make Moses's job even more difficult (see Exodus 10:1 as one example of this). Why would God work in opposition to the leader that he had called to emancipate his people?

22. It could be argued that our wounds are inflicted by the fallen world we live in, not by God. Does God give us a limp, or does he merely allow us to be broken by the world in which we live? Explain your answer.

23. When God renamed Jacob, he gave him the name Israel, meaning "one who has wrestled with God." If God were to rename you, what word or phrase might he use? If you were to rename yourself, what word or phrase would you use? Why would you choose that name?

Limping leaders know their weakness, but they are not weak. There is no shame in being in a power position, nor should anyone feel guilty about success. There are many instances where God blesses his followers with power and success. The danger, of course, comes when a leader gives too much credit to himself.

In his book *Moses on Management,* David Baron illustrates how Moses learned not to be blinded by his own power.

> After God appeared to Moses in the burning bush, after He dispensed with Moses' objections and laid out His plan to free the slaves, He threw in something else almost as an afterthought. "I, however, will stiffen [Pharaoh's] heart so that he will not let the people go." This sentence has perplexed many readers. If God was all-powerful and wanted the Israelites to escape Egypt, why didn't he *soften* Pharaoh's heart?[2]

God knew that his miracles and signs would be much more significant if he worked through Moses to defeat the *hardened* heart of the world's most powerful political leader.

Baron continues,

> When Moses first told Pharaoh of the Lord's instruction to "let My people go," Pharaoh's response was, "Who is the Lord that I should heed him and let Israel go? I do not know the Lord, nor will I let Israel go." His arrogance prevented him from taking Moses seriously, not only on the first day, but year after year, plague after plague.... Therein lies the lesson. A leader that arrogant, that tied to the old ways, that cut off from the events around him, will not be aware that the nation is lost. A leader who is all-powerful will often bring down his own society. What Moses learned from Pharaoh, and what all successful managers must bear in mind, is that the more isolated and arrogant a leader becomes, the less able he is to see the big picture clearly and act rationally.[3]

It is all too easy to fall into the trap of arrogance and the trumpeting of our power. If Pharaoh had given in to Moses's initial demand, Moses might have set off into the wilderness with the same level of arrogance he had seen in the Hebrews' former captor. But God hardened Pharaoh's heart and seemingly set Moses up for failure in order to build into Moses the power of a limping leader.

THE GLORY OF LEADERSHIP

As we count the cost of leadership, it's crucial that we also factor in the cost of glory. The greatest glory we can know is to see Jesus' life planted in a heart, then watch beauty and righteousness begin to grow. But it's not easy to be the person invited into God's glory. We relish our place at God's glorious feast, but then we are called to engage an even greater difficulty. Glory casts us not into ease but into the arms of a relentless God who desires for us to know even greater glory.

God is playing out his plot in order to entice reluctant and troubled servants who, in being humbled as leaders, are lifted up to see his glory.

3

NOTHING SUCCEEDS
LIKE IMPERFECTION

Those who lead with a limp become familiar with two inescapable truths of broken and effective leadership. First, a leader must recognize and openly acknowledge that she is the organization's chief sinner. Second, leading begins with desire. This second point may seem to conflict with our first chapter on the subject of reluctance, but desire and reluctance actually go hand in hand. We are not talking about blind desire, but rather the innate desire to lead even if we are reluctant in doing so.

In chapter 4 of *Leading with a Limp,* I (Dan) tell the story of Paul Steinke, a student leader at Mars Hill Graduate School. Paul led the student council with power that came from his broken leadership. A popular professor had resigned, and the school's attorney counseled the faculty and administration to say nothing. In the vacuum of silence, rumors and accusations abounded.

By midsummer almost the entire student leadership team of eight men and women were on the verge of resigning. When I returned to campus after a vacation, I received an invitation to meet with them. Some faculty members believed that such a meeting would only create more division. Remember, we had not met earlier because we had been told not to speak about the professor's resignation. On the other hand, if the student council members left the school, I seriously doubted whether our young graduate school could survive.

The night of the meeting I encountered an amazing sight. In the meeting room stood a beautiful table set with candles and freshly cut flowers. The students had decided to serve us dinner.

I had come prepared for hurt, anger, and accusations. I was not at all prepared for humility, kindness, and invitation. As the group began to eat, Paul spoke:

> As students we are here with a great deal of hurt and confusion. Some are angry. Some have made the decision to leave the school. Others are in the middle of making a decision about their future, but we all have realized that in our heartache none of us have come to you to ask: how are you? Whether you have failed or not, we have failed you by not opening our hearts to you and asking what you have endured through these events. We want to ask you to tell your stories, sharing to the degree you wish.[1]

I nearly started weeping. When he finished speaking, I thanked Paul, and then I tried to name the fear, the fury, and the soul-deadening silence I had felt subjected to bear in the wake of the professor's resignation. Each faculty representative spoke, and we also heard the stories of the students. There were tears and unexpected laughter. We weren't able to say everything we wanted, but we had finally heard one another's pain and confusion.

In such a situation it would have been far too easy for Paul or any other leader to be disappointed, angry, or cynical. Instead, Paul allowed himself to dream and to risk—and that requires the willingness to not run from desire. To hold on to desire in the face of possible defeat requires a courage that arises from a heart unafraid of failure. And a limping leader has little to fear because he has embraced a far deeper failure than whatever happens on the surface of life. He has embraced a failure of love—his failure to fully love God and people—that can be healed only by the forgiving kindness of Jesus.

Paul Steinke led in power from a position of desire and in acknowledgment of his status as chief among sinners. All are sinners, of course, but a limping leader takes her place at the head of the line.

Think about how this story from chapter 4 of *Leading with a Limp* applies to you and your organization. To help prompt your thinking, answer the following questions. Later, if possible, discuss these questions with the members of your leadership team, committee, faculty, ministry team, or staff.

1. If you were the head of the seminary in this situation, what would you have done differently? For example, would you have ignored the counsel of your attorney *not* to discuss the professor's resignation? Would you have accepted the student council's invitation? What would you have said after Paul Steinke spoke? Explain your answer.

2. At the meeting hosted by the student council, would you have let your emotions show? Why or why not? Do you think it is wise for a leader to be vulnerable and show emotions in front of colleagues or staff? Why or why not?

3. As you read about the meeting between the student leadership and the seminary leaders, which of these thoughts did you have? First circle the response that most closely matches your own. Then write down why you felt that way. If you are using this workbook with a group, talk about which responses people chose and why.

    a. *I never would have let it get that far.*

    b. *Decisions are tough. Change is tough. Time will eventually heal the hurt.*

    c. *I wish I had some subordinates like Paul in my organization. I doubt anyone would ever do that for me.*

    d. *What Paul did was wonderful, but it didn't change the fact that the leadership was advised not to discuss the matter.*

    e. Other thought. Write it here: _____

_____

As I (Matt) read Dan's accounts, I am struck by how quickly leaders can give in to an innate desire for self-protection. Faced with untenable circumstances, we want to pull back into a defensive posture when reaching out is actually needed most. In this instance, Paul led from a place of brokenness. He overcame his natural desire for safety and chose servanthood instead. He not only accomplished his own objectives but also provided an example of leadership for the entire graduate school—students and staff alike—and moved the organization forward.

As you think more about Dan's story, consider whether you have created an environment that elicits in others a desire both to follow you and reach out to you. Showing weakness does not make you weak. It makes you real.

BEING THE CHIEF SINNER

Christ Jesus came into the world to save sinners—of whom I am the worst.
But for that very reason I was shown mercy so that in me, the worst of sinners,
Christ Jesus might display his unlimited patience as an example for those who
would believe on him and receive eternal life. (1 Timothy 1:15–16)

With these words, Paul is calling leaders to be desperate and honest and to be so
transparent that others would say they know us well. If your mind immediately pic-
tures a so-called leader who is more complaining than conquering, more personal stories than personal guidance, then you are misunderstanding Paul's intention. When we
lead from a place of weakness, we are not abandoning leadership. We are, however,
making it clear that we do not view ourselves as better than anyone else. Honesty and
transparency create a desire in those around us to follow our leadership.

4. Take a few moments to write down some ways you could increase your level
   of transparency, honesty, and storytelling. Put a star next to the weakness
   that would be most difficult to admit to your staff.

When you choose to be transparent, you have an opportunity to alter the way you
are perceived. Freely admitting your chief-sinner status shows that you are honest and
that you want what is best for the organization. As those around you get to know your
story, they will also begin to appreciate what has shaped you in the past and what may
shape you in the future.

But don't try to move from no self-disclosure to full disclosure in one fell swoop.

You can't simply get out of bed tomorrow morning and say, "I'm going to take a whole new approach to leadership. Today I'm going to call everyone into the conference room and tell them my story!" Although that might be helpful, it might also cause your staff to wonder what you've been drinking. You can, however, take a gradual and very deliberate approach to transparency.

5. As you look back at the way you have worked with your staff, have you embraced or resisted opportunities to use stories from your life as discussion points? Explain why you have chosen either the path of vulnerability or the path of silence.

6. As you now prepare to start telling your story, first consider your recent past. Recall the meetings you led or participated in during the last two weeks. When might you have been more forthright in your comments? in your guidance of the meeting? in your responses to your staff?

7. As you think back over the past two weeks, when might you have taken advantage of opportunities to use your own struggles as discussion points?

Desire Versus Success

Once you begin to grasp both the power of making it known that you are your organization's chief sinner and the importance of doing so, it's time to tap into desire to fuel your effectiveness. Even when you feel like the world's most reluctant leader, desire keeps you in the game.

But realize this about desire: *there is a major difference between never being satisfied and always looking to improve.* Those who are never satisfied tend to demoralize and eventually demotivate their staff. Most of us have been around never-satisfied leaders, and we understand the motivation to find the nearest exit. But contrast that with the leader who is on a quest to always improve. The leader who wholeheartedly desires improvement celebrates her organization's successes, but she also can't wait to look at new ways to make it even better: "Let's celebrate together—and then let's look to the future." This is a limping leader.

In my part-time role as a church worship director, I (Matt) meet every week with a worship planning team so we can analyze recent services and discuss upcoming ones. Members of the team offer what they believe is their absolute best to these meetings. However, at the end of each meeting we ask one final question: "What can we do to build on everything we've discussed tonight to make it *even better?* What's the one thing we haven't yet thought of?"

Once in a while we come up with a new idea that becomes an integral part of the next worship service. In fact, in many instances the implemented idea is eventually seen as one of the most important new elements in our times of worship.

8. Think about the desires that fuel your passion as a leader. What is the primary desire that keeps you in the game when you face opposition, are fearful of failure, or are tempted to question your calling? What about that particular desire resonates with you as a leader?

9. What are the differences between never being satisfied and always looking to improve? Think of a leader you have served who was never satisfied. What impact did this approach to leadership have on you? Be specific.

10. Now think of a leader you have served who was always looking to improve. What impact did this approach to leadership have on you? Be specific.

11. Once again think for a moment about your own desires as a leader and your leadership style. Does your primary desire prompt you to lean more toward never being satisfied or toward always looking to improve? In what ways does that leaning surface in the way you lead? In what ways does that leaning surface in the stories you tell from your own life?

12. If you have a colleague whom you trust, ask that person to answer the preceding questions about either your leaning toward never being satisfied or your way of always looking to improve. What do your colleague's observations reveal about your leadership?

4

WHAT IT TAKES
TO FACE CRISIS

Whether you thrive on crisis or curse it, if you're a leader you can't avoid it. The prospect of leading your organization through chaos may energize you, and when the crises keep coming, they can also exhaust you. Even so, it's your job to deal with chaos.

1. Think about the biggest crisis you have faced as a leader, specifically a crisis that impacted you personally. As you look back on that time, list five ways in which you felt broken by the crisis.

   a.

   b.

   c.

   d.

   e.

2. Now think about the biggest crisis that has threatened your organization. As you searched for the best way to lead your people through that time, what lasting effects did that experience have on you as a leader? List the top five ways in which you felt broken by the process:

a.

b.

c.

d.

e.

Reluctant leaders are well aware of the false promises of power, pride, and ambition, and that's one reason why they're effective during a crisis. Knowing that these conventional trappings of leadership are not equal to the challenges of crises, reluctant leaders are actually in a better position to confront crisis and not be defeated by it. When leaders are already familiar with their brokenness, guiding others through chaos is easier for them. During a crisis, limping leaders are able to draw from their resources of courage, depth, gratitude, openness, and hope. They have embraced the lessons learned in similar situations in their pasts. This is why they're effective when chaos reigns.

3. Think again about the biggest crisis you have faced as a leader that impacted you personally. As you look back again on that time, describe the ways in which you drew strength from courage, depth, gratitude, openness, or hope.

4. Think again about the biggest crisis that has threatened your organization. As you led your people through that time, in what specific ways did you tap into the resources of courage, depth, gratitude, openness, or hope?

BATTLE SCARS

No one—even leaders who already know they are broken—comes through a crisis completely unscathed. But are you thankful for the battle wounds you have suffered, or are you careful not to think about them too much? Consider these lyrics from "Break My Heart" by Kathy Troccoli:

It's in the pain
That I have grown
Through all the sorrow
I have known
But, if that's what it takes
For You to lead me this far
Go ahead and break my heart[1]

Many of us leaders have uttered the words "If that's what it takes." But how many of us have prayed that phrase and followed it with "Go ahead, Lord, break my heart"? It's important to remember that such a request is not a sign of weakness. Quite the opposite: in our weakness and brokenness we find new sources of strength.

As the crisis unfolds and we rely on these new sources of strength, we must not lose sight of our commitment, our passion, and our calling. And that's too easy to do, even in the church. More than 90 percent of the leaders who responded to our leadership survey are involved in church ministry. Where else are human beings asked to give so much of themselves? Where else is it so important to model a Christlike approach to the leadership conundrum, to constantly cast vision, and to live totally in the present? And in what other leadership endeavor is there more crisis?

If you work in Christian ministry, we'd be surprised if you don't identify with this confession from Carlo Carretto:

> How baffling you are, oh Church, and yet how I love you!
> How you have made me suffer, and yet how much I owe you!
> I should like to see you destroyed, and yet I need your presence.
> You have given me so much scandal and yet you have made me understand sanctity.
> I have seen nothing in the world more devoted to obscurity, more compromised, more false, and I have touched nothing more pure, more generous, more beautiful. How often I have wanted to shut the doors of my soul in your face, and how often I have prayed to die in the safety of your arms.
> No, I cannot free myself from you, because I am you, although not completely. And where should I go?[2]

The crises of leadership are intensified by the contradictions of ministry. Our consideration of the constancy of crisis as well as the contradictory demands placed on us as leaders take us to another crucial aspect of leading in times of crisis: resolve.

RESOLVE IN THE FACE OF CRISIS

In times of major crisis, it's an advantage if you've been taught by past brokenness. Broken leaders tend to be humble leaders, and humility is a strength when you're forced to deal with crisis. But some broken leaders do not become great leaders. One reason is that they have failed to develop the resolve they need.

In chapter 5 of *Leading with a Limp,* a pastor named Lee describes a major crisis he faced when his church lost a large number of people—many of them the church's leaders and most generous financial supporters.

> Up to one-half of our church community was going to be leaving us in the span of three months. They were moving on to new jobs or grad school, or they were leaving due to graduation. Not only were we losing a significant percentage of our church membership, but the people who were moving represented leadership in almost every area of our community as well as a large percentage of our financial base. We faced the very real possibility of having to shut down simply for lack of people to carry out what needed to be accomplished. My first response was to curl up in a fetal position in the corner and wait for the end.[3]

Many of us have gone straight to that corner in far less demanding situations. But others face into the crisis and do whatever it takes. Why the difference?

5. Think about the biggest crisis you are facing right now. What was your initial reaction to the situation? Was it more like hiding in a corner and licking your wounds or standing up and shouting into the face of the storm?

6. In what situation, if ever, have you initially responded to a crisis by denying the problem or hiding from the issue and then gone against this natural bent and walked the "whatever it takes" course? If you have, what brought about the radical change in your response?

COURAGE: THE THRESHOLD TO OVERCOMING CRISIS

What keeps effective leaders standing when others who have just as much drive lose heart? To help you answer that question, let's look at another case study in limping leadership.

The year is approximately 1400 BC. One of the most gifted of all limping leaders has died. Moses left behind a fickle nation—God's chosen people are constantly in need of reminders of God's faithfulness.

Joshua is the new leader, chosen by God and charged to be strong and courageous. God assures Joshua: "I am with you as I was with Moses" (Joshua 3:7). Joshua calls together the people and tells them that in three days he will lead them across the Jordan River. Imagine the setting. Moses is gone and suddenly here's Joshua saying, "Have no fear. God is with us, and we move out soon!" He explains that as soon as the feet of the Levitical priests carrying the Ark of the Covenant touch the water, the river will stop flowing and the people will pass over into the land that God has promised them.

On the morning of the river crossing, the people set out with great anticipation and probably a great deal of fear as well. The priests arrive first at the river's edge, look at Joshua for a shot of encouragement, and step into the water. Keep in mind that the priests are carrying the Ark of the Covenant, which represented God's presence with the people. It's the time of harvest and the river is overflowing its banks. But as soon as the priests' feet touched the water, the Scriptures tell us, the water stops and rises in a heap at a city called Adam (see Joshua 3:16). Downstream from that point the river continues to flow toward the Red Sea.

Here is an interesting fact that is not often highlighted: the city of Adam was approximately thirty miles upstream from the point where Joshua and the Israelites were set to cross the river. It is safe to assume that the priests, once they stepped into the river, had to wait for thirty miles' worth of river to move past them on its way to the sea. Even with the swiftest current, how long would it take for thirty miles of water to pass by and expose the riverbed? Thirty minutes? Sixty? Ninety? The Israelites would have been familiar with the account of the parting of the Red Sea years earlier in their history. In that case, the event was a true parting of the waters. But on the banks of the Jordan River, the situation was entirely new—and far from clear-cut.

7. Put yourself in Joshua's place. The man who led the exodus is dead, and you're now the guy in charge. You've told the nation of Israel that God wants them all to cross this river and that God will take care of the water. What are you feeling at this point?

8. Would you begin to question whether you had heard God correctly? Or would you try to explain to the people why the priests were in the water and the river was still flowing past them? Give the reasons for your choice.

Joshua is no stranger to taking risks, and his track record shows him to be a man of faith and a man of integrity. But here he is waxing on about guidance from God while the priests are standing in the water, and it's plain for all to see that the river continues to rush past their ankles. How long do you think it took before someone said, "Hey, Joshua! Are you sure about the instructions God gave you? You haven't been doing this for that long, you know. Maybe you heard him wrong."

Another fifteen minutes pass. The priests are getting restless. "Are you going to take responsibility if we drop this thing, Joshua?" The priests consider stepping back onto the riverbank. Joshua prays earnestly to God but doesn't panic. He musters more courage and waits.

9. At this juncture Joshua probably feels the need to reassure the people. If you were in his place, what would you do to convince your followers that you had in fact heard from God and that this is indeed what God has told you to do?

We don't know what Joshua did to reassure the doubters. But we do know that eventually everyone crossed safely over to the land that God had promised their forefathers. We also can infer that the Israelites, although quite prone to complaint, did not rebel against Joshua. We know from their history that the Hebrews weren't afraid to question their leaders. And they had shown in the past that they were quick to lose faith when circumstances seemed to go against them. This time, though, they followed their new leader even though thirty miles of water had to flow past before exposing the riverbed.

What made Joshua such an effective leader that crises were present but divisions were not? We can't say for sure, but knowing his character and his approach to leadership, we can conclude that courage and humility had much to do with his effectiveness. And we can add to those essentials his level of transparency. Joshua told the people all that God had told him. He didn't hedge his bets by tossing in a "Just trust me" at the end of his speech. He laid out the facts, encouraged the people, gave them a time line, then sounded the call to cross the river.

10. Think of a time when you had to lead your staff or organization forward when they were reluctant to go due to circumstances that seemed to contradict your vision. What did you do to instill confidence and lead your people? (Or, looking back, what could you have done?)

11. In addition to being courageous, Joshua demonstrated humility and transparency. In what ways do courage, humility, and transparency manifest themselves in the life and work of a leader? If you are using this workbook in a group, discuss your answers.

5

THE PROBLEM OF COMPLEXITY

Complexity takes us deeper into the reality of leading with a limp. Think about your world as a leader and all the things that are not predictable, all the decisions that are not clear-cut, and all the competing demands and interests that you have to take into account. The uncertainty and ambiguity that come with such complexity convince many leaders that they must meet the challenge with an equally complex strategy.

But does the challenge of complexity really require greater complexity on the part of the leader? Or should we take exactly the opposite approach by getting back to the fundamentals of limping leadership? Can the essentials of courage, depth, gratitude, openness, and hope stand up to the dizzying degree of complexity that you confront as a leader? Put another way, is all this talk about the power of reluctant, broken leadership a pipe dream—something that's interesting to talk about but really has nothing to offer in the real world?

We'd be surprised if you haven't asked these questions already. They are crucial questions, and we're confident that limping leadership is the best answer.

The Origins of Chaos

In chapter 6 of *Leading with a Limp*, I (Dan) talk about the importance of the past, present, and future when we confront complexity. Let's look again at how each of these affects our approach to complexity.

The Past

The past provides each of us with a grid that we use to interpret new data. Complexity arises when the existing grids from the past seem to be breaking down or when another grid competes for ascendancy. For example, a member of your staff needs to be fired, but you have emphasized relationship in your dealings with staff. Other staff members become insecure whenever a co-worker is let go. After all, they could be next in line for dismissal. You make the hard but necessary decision to let the staff member go, and then you endure the objections: "I thought you were committed to relationships!" or "I thought we were like a family." If relationships are primary, how do you justify firing an employee for the good of the organization?

1. If you've been in leadership very long, you've had to fire someone. Think about the most difficult firing decision you've made. In the space below, write down the primary factors that made that decision and its implementation a complex matter.

2. What did you tell your staff about why letting the person go was the best course of action? What were the primary objections to your decision to fire the person?

The past adds layers of complexity when your existing schema is challenged by the current demands of leadership. That's why every leader needs to constantly ask, "What lens am I using to read reality in any given moment?"

The Present

The present adds complexity when we use a grid from the past to "see" in the present because that grid shapes what we see and how we see it. We tend to see only what our grid from the past has predisposed us to see.

3. Think of a time when you faced a leadership challenge and initially saw only a few of the many factors affecting the situation. What did you do to broaden your field of vision as you addressed the challenge?

No one sees everything she needs to see. We all see through our own lens, so we must ask questions that broaden our vision:

- What am I not seeing in this situation?
- What grid am I imposing on my world that keeps me from seeing more completely?
- What bias from my ethnic, socioeconomic, religious, or experiential grids is blinding me to my current situation?

Asking yourself these questions will help you recognize how you automatically assess situations and how you typically view the people in a given situation. Realize, too, that your grid is not only selective (it narrows your vision), but it also introduces value judgments. Your grid compels you to see certain data as primary and other things as less important. We don't see all that is present right in front of us, and what we do see is often distorted by the bias introduced by our grid.

4. Think of a time when new data introduced ambiguity by contradicting your earlier assumptions or conclusions, but resulted in a better solution. What caused you to be open to the new information and factor it into your decision?

The Future

The future, by definition, is the great unknown. It's unpredictable, uncertain, unclear. It makes us uncomfortable because it introduces uncertainty.

Leading your organization into the future requires that you see reality through a new lens. Yes, just as you're hoping to get chaos under control, you are asked to switch lenses—which introduces even greater chaos. Leading others requires depth and breadth of perception (that's where the new lens helps), and broader perception provides more data, increases your options, and gives you more tools to use in addressing chaos and complexity. Such an approach does little to clarify ambiguity or to rid the future of uncertainty. But it does increase your chances of making the best decision.

5. Stop for a moment and ask yourself, "If I knew in advance that my decisions would meet with success and that my strategies would result in the growth and health of my organization, what would I change about the way I lead?" Write your answer here.

6. Although the future will always be uncertain, what keeps you from leading your organization forward with the same level of confidence you would have if you knew in advance that your plans would succeed?

We leaders hate uncertainty because we hate feeling out of control. We can't read the future with 20/20 vision, so we question whether we're making the best decisions as measured by some external standard. That is the inevitable complexity that is introduced by the future.

ENTERING THE COMPLEXITY OF THE FUTURE

The more complex the situation, the more we tend to resort to analysis. To analyze something means to dissect it until we come to an understanding that allows us to predict, manage, and even control the problem. But chaos theory tells us that every effort to measure, let alone control, a phenomenon not only changes it but also moves it in an unpredictable direction.

Instead of analysis and the resulting actions, leaders need to dance with the chaos. Dancing with the confounding complexity of leading an organization requires the conviction that deep, invisible patterns of order—patterns that are independent of our control—can be found. And the only way to find them is through an active surrender to nuance, mystery, and surprise.

7. In the space below, list the top three projects and/or decisions that currently occupy your best thinking and most concentrated effort. Next to each project or decision, write down the primary factors contributing to the complexity.

    a.

    b.

    c.

8. What percentage of your work on each of the three involves trying to control the situation or attempting to make the outcome as predictable as possible? Does your effort help or hinder your ability to lead effectively?

We would agree that it's not a bad thing to attempt to control chaos. After all, leadership is more than just vision casting. The people in your organization look to you to make confident, effective decisions. The danger, however, lies in relying on a rigid, dogmatic cloud of your own making; you don't want to control chaos by limiting your options. If you close yourself off from new data or developments that may completely alter the course of your preferred approach, then you are making yourself a less competent leader. You must never allow a grid that you developed in the past to blind you to the present or prevent you from dealing effectively with the future. As you seek the best decision possible, always be open to new interpretations of the events around you. Chaos can never be controlled by closing off your options.

DON'T IGNORE CONFLICTING DATA

When we are grounded in our relationship with God, we have a tendency to think that our personal convictions become completely his. This belief causes us to cut ourselves off from additional information and input that we desperately need if we are to lead effectively.

Being convinced of the rightness of our biases reminds me of fans of opposing football teams. Consider this scenario: It's down to the final two minutes of the game, and a field goal will clinch the win for the team that now has the ball. No one knows what the outcome will be, and players on both sidelines can be seen in silent prayer. The clock ticks too slowly for the team that's ahead—and much too quickly for the team that has the ball and is trying desperately to score. When the game ends, half the stadium erupts in elation at the victory. Players and fans on that side can be seen saying a quick "Thank you, God!" Meanwhile, fans wearing the losing team's colors are despondent over the outcome.

Now, what just happened? Were the prayers that went up from the winning teams' bleachers uttered with greater conviction? The fans and players on both sides of the stadium are people of passion and firm belief, and both groups are convinced of the rightness of their cause. But only one team won the game.

Here's the point: It's one thing to try to convince those around you to support your strongly held conviction. But you do yourself and your organization a great injustice if you ignore the input and feedback of those who disagree with you. Couching your personal conviction in the terminology and paradigm of "acting on God's will" can turn the outcome against you. And it can hinder the spiritual growth of those around you. In the game some praying leaders win—and some lose.

9. Think about a time when your convictions as a leader conflicted with those held by your staff. What did you do about the contradictory data and conflicting values?

10. When, if ever, have you addressed complexity by closing yourself off from new data that conflicted with your bias? Did limiting your options make you a more effective leader, or did it hinder your effectiveness? In what ways?

11. Think about a time when you broadened your vision to include input or feedback that you had initially refused to embrace but later gave equal consideration. Did taking this step help you arrive at a better decision than you could have otherwise? Explain.

6

Gratitude in the Face of Betrayal

I n this chapter we're taking a very different approach to the material. We're going to look at how a small discussion group might deal with issues related to betrayal as they are presented in chapter 7 of *Leading with a Limp*. Imagine yourself participating in this discussion. As you join in, let it clarify your thoughts and broaden your understanding of the inevitable betrayals that accompany leadership. (To refresh your memory, read chapter 7 of *Leading with a Limp* before tackling this workbook chapter.)

SPEAKING OF BETRAYAL

Leader: That chapter on betrayal hit close to home. Did anyone else think immediately about instances of envy, betrayal, and narcissism? Did reading chapter 7 cause you to relive personal encounters with these leadership challenges?

To get started, let's think about applicable Scripture passages. What are some verses that deal directly with either envy, betrayal, or narcissism—since these issues are interconnected? In chapter 7 Dan Allender mentioned verses in Ecclesiastes 4 that deal with oppression as well as Jonah's self-righteous attitude that made him refuse initially to obey God's call to lead. Speaking personally, I loved the analogy of Ralph Lauren being asked to be a greeter at Wal-Mart. Brilliant.

Who has a verse to share?

Bill: Proverbs 3:31 says, "Do not envy a man of violence and do not choose any of his ways" (ESV).

Josh: I would hope we're not doing that. There are enough nutzoids in the world as it is, without other people wanting to take their cues from violent leaders.

Leader: Very true, although I wouldn't be so quick to assume that we never envy disreputable people. Let's keep as open a mind as possible, even when some interpretations might at first seem ridiculous. Who else has a verse?

Susan: First Corinthians 13:4, of course: "[Love] does not envy, it does not boast." Love is God. Love is Jesus. Jesus does not envy or boast, and we are supposed to do all we can to live like that, to represent him in our lives.

Leader: That's a perfect verse for what we're talking about. But how does it fit your responsibilities as a leader?

Susan: Honestly, the gist of that verse seems so naive—like third-grade Sunday school—when I think of the realities I face as a leader. If I'm honest about it, the simplicity of Scripture seems unreal to me and unrelated to my situation at work.

Leader: As the rest of you think about the things you face in your work as leaders, do you feel that the teaching in 1 Corinthians 13 misses the point? Are you looking for something more detailed—or perhaps more nuanced—to adequately address the layers of betrayal and narcissism that you encounter?

Mark: I know exactly what Susan is referring to. If I'm coming off a weekend that was fabulous for my family, relaxing for me, and a great learning time at church, the biblical concepts are as clear as could be on Monday morning. But as soon as a crisis hits or, even more so, a betrayal happens like the examples described in the book, I feel a tendency to set that belief framework aside and deal with the immediate problem. I know that's the opposite of what I should do, but it seems to happen anyway.

Bill: I know what you mean. My insecurities surface rapidly in times of crisis, and I find myself gravitating to past behaviors.

Let's take a break from the group discussion and ask some personal questions:

1. What was your reaction to Susan's observation that the directness and simplicity of Scripture often seem out of touch with the hard reality that leaders face? Describe a specific example from your life as a leader, if you can.

2. Which speaker do you identify with most: Bill, Josh, Susan, or Mark? What did that person say that especially rings true with your experience as a leader?

3. What scriptures provide direction for suffering the betrayal every leader faces?

THE SCARS OF LEADERSHIP

Leader: Betrayal scars us and shapes us, and because of that, it deserves serious analysis. What were some points that jumped out at you as you read chapter 7 of *Leading with a Limp?*

Lisa: This statement: "No good deed goes unpunished."

Josh: I loved that. It's so true!

Lisa: All laughter aside, it really did get me thinking. I suppose betrayal, by definition, is unexpected when it occurs. And there is that feeling of it being so undeserved. On the other hand, when I feel I haven't done my best and I am faced with betrayal, I don't react the same way. I really hit the brick wall of betrayal when I feel like I've been doing a bang-up job and then—*wham!*—betrayal strikes. This probably makes me the prime candidate for "most self-righteous."

Mark: Join the team.

Leader: So you're saying that betrayal stings the most when it comes in the wake of good deeds or superior performance. That makes sense. Can you offer any specific examples?

Josh: I've got one. Last year I was looking for some ways to further motivate my team by bringing everyone closer together. I scheduled a full-day retreat, and there I encouraged each person to share a personal struggle as a way for us to see both the humanness of each individual and our need to support one another. I started the discussion, and I shared some of my struggles as a leader, specifically some of the struggles in our current organization. I even admitted some of my mistakes in past staffing decisions.

During the same retreat I told my team that I was completely content in my current position, but I was no different from anyone else in that I wanted to always be open to new opportunities. Looking back on it, I realize that saying that might have been unwise. In this case, it led to betrayal.

A month later, when one of the staff members left the organization, a board member asked him about his reasons for leaving. The employee mentioned my admission, telling them I said I wasn't sure I would stay with the organization. Not only was that a gross misrepresentation, but by the time I had a chance to respond, the board had already met to discuss my alleged comments. I eventually was able to provide a complete explanation, but I'm not sure the seed of doubt ever fully left their minds. To this day I don't know why the employee did that, and I must admit it makes me wary about showing too much brokenness in front of my staff.

Leader: I understand your hesitation after that kind of betrayal. Dan Allender also points out that going overboard in confessing our failures and brokenness has the potential to lead to self-absorption and narcissism in addition to betrayal.

Susan: I'm glad you mentioned narcissism. I've always thought of that as a psychosocial disorder leading to predatory behavior and acts of violence.

Leader: Well, let's look at how Allender defines it. In chapter 7 he identifies four aspects of narcissism: showing a lack of interest in other people's perspectives, being highly opinionated, remaining emotionally detached, and operating in a way that is ruthlessly utilitarian. That's not us, right? Or are we sometimes wolves in sheep's clothing? Who can think of a narcissistic boss from a past experience—and I don't want everyone to talk at once!

Lisa: I once worked for a man who was the walking epitome of the adage: "If I want your opinion, I'll give it to you." I was expected to produce great results, but like an obsessed perfectionist father, he was never pleased with my work.

I laugh now when I think back to one of my annual performance reviews. My boss asked me if there was anything I would like to discuss, anything that might be hindering growth in my position and the success of the company. I mentioned that I felt stymied any time I wanted to present an idea or project that differed from his ideas. You won't believe how he responded! He said I was obviously not ready to be a leader if I questioned my own ability while, at the same time, not trusting those above me in the organization. My own comment was identified as the biggest negative of my annual review. He played off it to challenge me to do better.

Once again take a break from the group discussion and ask yourself a few questions:

4. Look again at the four traits of narcissistic leaders: lack of interest in other people's perspectives, highly opinionated, emotionally detached, and ruthlessly utilitarian. Think of a leader you have worked with who exhibited one or more of these characteristics. In what ways did that tendency end up being a betrayal of you and your leadership in that organization?

5. When, if ever, have you been guilty of any of the characteristics of narcissism in your work as a leader? Which characteristic did you display? What was the outcome of your narcissistic behavior? What was the effect on your staff? on your organization?

6. If you are using this workbook with a group, discuss the four characteristics of narcissism and let each person share about an experience working for a narcissist or being a narcissist.

THE POWER OF GRATITUDE

Leader: The failings of Lisa's former boss are obvious. However, this may be a good time to go back to Josh's earlier comment that none of us would ever choose to envy the "man of violence" referred to in Proverbs 3:31 (ESV). Lisa's boss was not physically violent, but I would venture to say that she felt a certain amount of envy, even though she despised the man. Any truth to that, Lisa?

Lisa: It's interesting that you ask, because even though I knew in my heart he was misguided, I envied his level of self-confidence. I wanted to make decisions that didn't cause me to wake up at 3:00 a.m., second-guessing myself and questioning my own judgment. I imagined what it would be like to be that unfeeling and that focused.

Leader: Many of us can relate. The man in your story had a tremendous ego, and our own egos cause us to be of two minds toward such narcissistic leaders. We despise and revere them at the same time. So what can bring us to a state of humility when those types of attacks come our way? Allender indicates that gratitude plays a big part. What do you think?

Mark: I don't know if this is what you're looking for, but I've been trying to be thankful not just for the good but also for the bad. Forgiveness certainly plays a part in that. But if I can somehow be thankful for the person who betrayed me, the boss who doesn't understand me, and the subordinates who criticize me, I get a glimpse of the bigger picture that I want to have take priority over my feelings about my work. The bigger goal is my becoming more like Christ. I know that I tend to take more time in prayer when I'm being attacked or frustrated. If I'm talking more with God in the midst of those challenges, then I should be thankful for them. It sounds a little self-righteous, I know, and I definitely have not achieved total success here, but I'm calmer when I act in this manner and, quite frankly, I think I'm a better leader when I do so.

Leader: Certainly nothing wrong with a successful example. That's what this workshop is all about.

Lisa: I'm thankful that it's not about me. Even on the days when I feel like it is, it isn't really. And there's freedom in that. Either I trust God—or I don't. I believe the gospel is a simple message; we're the ones who make our lives complicated. I'm so thankful that, at the end of the day, it's only about Jesus. That truth keeps things in perspective, even when they get tough.

Leader: Well, we've run out of time. Thanks for coming, and I pray that each of us will realize that the answers of limping leadership lie in the winding journey of life and in our willingness to analyze our own hearts.

Now that you have read the discussion, once again take a few moments to ask yourself some questions.

7. Mark just suggested that gratitude is a right response to the betrayal of others. He reasoned that being betrayed hurts and that the hurt drives him to God in prayer. Comment on his perspective. Do you agree with his suggestion? Why or why not?

8. Mark also stated his opinion that the purpose of leadership is not to advance in his career or to achieve better results for his organization but to become more Christlike. Do you agree? Why or why not?

9. If you are using this workbook in a group, let each person comment on the value of gratitude as a response to betrayal. Also discuss Christlikeness as the goal of leadership.

7

THE OPENNESS
THAT COMBATS LONELINESS

The year was 1993, and I (Matt) found myself on a nine-seat turboprop plane flying through heavy fog to the town of Page, Arizona. A storm was tossing about the small plane as if it were a toy, and I was turning a new shade of green as I tried to control my rocking stomach. Two hours later, still on the edge of losing my lunch, I was boarding a houseboat on Lake Powell. It was the middle of January, not the vacation season. We were already cold and damp, and we hadn't even left the dock.

I was there with several colleagues and a sizable crew, embarking on a four-day adventure through the inner channels of this massive lake. We would be filming a music video as well as doing the main photo shoot for an album release. I was twenty-seven years old, and this was the first time I'd be listed as the executive producer of a major project. We'd already finished recording the album, and now it was time for the other elements of the product push.

It was an interesting paradox as I realized that I was young enough to make a few mistakes but old enough that they'd better not be big ones. We had a top video director, an expert photographer, an incredible marketing mind from the record company, and one of the top-selling Christian recording artists of all time. Yet I still felt apprehension and a certain loneliness in my spirit. I prayed that I wouldn't mess up anything.

Lake Powell is one of the planet's most beautiful man-made phenomena. Although the two thousand miles of rugged coastline and massive rock formations were made by the master Creator, the lake didn't appear until the Glen Canyon Dam was constructed. (Some interesting trivia is attached to the lake. For instance, part of the set for the MGM classic *The Greatest Story Ever Told* now lies underwater. My friend's walkie-talkie is also at the bottom of the lake, but that's another story.)

Since we were there in the middle of January, no one else was on the lake. We felt as if we were heading into a great, silent unknown. But by the second day, work was going pretty well. The marketing director and I volunteered to run the fog machine, which was necessary for visual effects on the video. We spent the day circling around in a powerboat, launching fog from an apparatus that promised to enshroud an area the size of a football field in less than thirty seconds. It was all great fun until I started getting sick—not seasick but sick with a respiratory virus. By that night my throat was on fire, and I opted to rest awhile in one of the houseboats.

The only people with me just then were two men from California who had been hired to run the sailboat that was being used in the shots. To say that these men were strange would be a huge understatement. They had brought a couple of cases of beer on board before we left the main pier. That night, while we were anchored at a nearby beach, they had apparently decided to see how much of that beer they could drink, and by the time they came back to the houseboat, they were sauced.

I had a fever and a cough, and it was obvious that I was sick. The bigger of the two guys looked like an over-the-hill WWF wrestler. He sauntered over to me and began asking questions about my condition. I remember thinking, *Someone shoot me…please.*

"When did the symptoms start?"

"I'll be fine. Really." *Please tell me this isn't happening.*

"I can help you if you tell me what's going on," he said, his breath smelling like last call at a seaside bar.

I looked at him as calmly as I could and said, "It's probably a cold. I'll just have to wait it out, you know?" *Wrong thing to say, apparently.*

"There's your problem!" His voice was getting louder. "You accepted the symptoms voluntarily instead of refusing them."

"Excuse me?"

"Our minds have control over an amazing number of things. God gives us the ability to accept his immediate healing. Look at my hands. You wouldn't have any way of knowing other than my telling you, but I have the divine gift of healing. Here, feel my hands. Go ahead. Feel them… Feel how warm they are? That's the power of God."

Before I knew it, the man had his hands around my throat and was asking me if I had the faith to be healed. You know those times when you mentally step back from your situation and analyze the circumstances? I did that. As if I were looking down from above, I saw myself, feverish and sick, on a boat in the middle of a lake, talking with a couple of drunk yokels, one of whom had his hands around my throat. Ah, life is rich.

"What exactly do you want me to do?" I asked the self-professed healer.

He looked at me as if I were a stupid child. "I want you to choose to be healed."

"Sorry," I said. "I don't think it works that way."

"You can feel the warmth of my hands, but you don't have enough faith in God to be healed?" He was really starting to bug me.

I asked him, "You're questioning my faith? What church do you belong to?"

"I don't need no church," he explained. "God and I have our own thing going."

Seeing that there was no way to win, especially since I was dealing with an inebriated self-taught healer, I simply said, "Thank you for your concern. I need to go lie down now, but I'm going to think about what you said."

I don't remember the "healer's" final words. I went into the back room where my bunk was, locked the door, and didn't come out until the next morning. I had plenty of bottled water at my bunk, but unfortunately the bathroom was in the front of the houseboat. Being sick and trying to stay hydrated, I needed to visit the facilities on a fairly frequent basis. The only way to get there, though, was to go past these two guys. I ended up using nature's chilly bathroom instead, accessed through the houseboat's back door.

I have never been as lonely as I was on that houseboat in the middle of Lake Powell on a Tuesday night in 1993. We eventually finished our work on the music video and made our way back to the marina. I checked into a warm and inviting lodge, ordered chicken soup, and enjoyed the longest hot shower of my life.

1. Sometimes leading gets more challenging when you're on the verge of a major breakthrough. Have you ever been struck with loneliness just before experiencing significant success? If so, tell the story in the space that follows. If not, share your thoughts on why loneliness might precede success.

2. When, if ever, has your loneliness been invaded by an unwanted guest? At that moment did you long more for a different choice of companion or merely for solitude? Why?

THE LONELINESS OF LEADERSHIP

Leadership can be very much like my experience on Lake Powell. As a leader you start off on a journey into a territory that looks much more perilous than you expected. You want very much to be "one of the guys," but the mantle of leadership brings with it a load of pressure and a sense of separation from everyone else involved in the project. You look around for someone to talk to, but you only see people who aren't interested in the things that concern you. To top it off, the people who do show an interest are the very ones you would prefer to stay away from. It is not a normal situation, and leaders are definitely not normal people.

3. Take a few minutes to write down your memories of a time when, as a leader, you felt a palpable loneliness that was closely related to your position as leader. Concentrate on your feelings of loneliness rather than the circumstances of leadership, unless they intertwine naturally.

   a. Describe the situation.

   b. What details of the situation produced your loneliness?

    c. Did you have anyone to confide in at the time? If so, who?

    d. Who tried to help you? And did those people really help, or did they merely add to your sense of being alone? Explain.

4. Write down your idea of the perfect helper in times of loneliness, in situations like the one you just described.

    Is there a person like this in your life right now? In what ways does this person specifically help you?

5. Now think about your current leadership situation. When you feel lonely, do you reach out to the person you just identified? If your helper is no longer around or you've never had such a helper, have you actively sought out someone to fill that role? Why or why not? What specific steps toward finding that person could you take?

HELP FOR LONELY LEADERS

As leaders we tend to rely on ourselves; we tend to do as much as possible without asking for help. This tendency can cause us to hide or deny our emotions and inner struggles. The buildup of crisis, complexity, and betrayal can also lead us to erect a wall in an attempt to protect ourselves and to help maintain our sanity in the chaos. But when loneliness strikes, as it always will, we find that the wall keeps out the very people who might spare us deeper loneliness. So in these times we can't ignore our need for other people.

Most leaders would agree that having close friendships and confidants makes us stronger. Many of those same people, however, will admit that finding time to cultivate such relationships is another matter. If we are to be effective leaders, heart-to-heart connection is key. One solution is fairly simple (though not necessarily easy): many of us just need to spend more time with our families.

6. Try this simple experiment: For a seven-day period dedicate yourself to getting every member of your family around the dinner table every night. If you live alone, do the same thing but with a friend or friends. If gathering for dinner is an absolute impossibility, then use the week to practice letting down your guard with colleagues.

Questions on Loneliness

7. Consider the following statements and classify each one as true or false in your life. Be honest!

    a. *I know how to have fun with my family.*

    b. *I can think of someone who would count me as his/her best friend.*

    c. *Within the last two weeks, I have had a frank conversation with another person concerning my emotions and struggles as a leader.*

    d. *No one truly understands me.*

    e. *Acquaintances or co-workers planning to go out for a meal or other activity know that I would go if they asked me.*

    f. *I fear that being honest and open with people at work could put my leadership position in jeopardy.*

    g. *I have fostered a community of care (for myself and others) in my workplace.*

The point of answering the preceding questions is to honestly examine the state of your relationships in light of your work. Every leader is different, as is every organization. However, the goal here is to start thinking about how you deal with loneliness when it hits.

Recognizing that you are in fact lonely is a beginning. Understanding why loneliness happens adds a few more pieces to the puzzle. But it is the practice of relational skills that will move you from isolation and loneliness to openness with others, and here are some skills to work on:

- Reach out.
- Share your stories.
- Don't bottle up your emotions.
- Acknowledge your struggles.
- Invest time and energy in other people.

One final note on my Lake Powell story: part of the intense loneliness I felt stemmed from the fact that I could not reach out to people who fueled my soul. This was before cell phones provided us ready access to anyone we might need to consult. In this instance I was out of touch for a week. Once I returned to the lodge at the end of the trip and talked to my wife on the phone, the intense emotion of the experience seemed far lighter, even kind of silly. I remember that whenever I need a light at the end of a dark, lonely tunnel.

Who are your lights at the end of the tunnel? If you don't have any, what will be your first step toward finding some?

8

The Weariness
That Invites Hope

At the time of this writing, I (Matt) am in Rangeley, Maine, enjoying a wonderful and rejuvenating vacation with my family. We have rented a log chalet, and in it we have put my family of four as well as my sister's family of four and my parents. Ten unique individuals, ten unique personalities, and a collection of ten bathroom idiosyncrasies.

It's actually going remarkably well. There's a lot to do in this small town, including listening to the Down East accents of the shop owners. When I order fresh Maine lobster and get ready to crack open that first leg, I want to hear that beautiful, "Ya got everything ya need theyah?" I love it.

There's a house down the road that's for sale. With kids who are still in elementary school, I think, *I could find a way to buy that as a vacation home and make money renting it and building up equity. Perfect!*

All I do is start to walk up the driveway as we stroll by, and my wife speaks a firm (and loud), "No!"

"Don't you just want to look at it, honey?"

"No!"

Ah, the wisdom of a caring spouse saving me from yet another disaster to add to my résumé of "surefire" ideas. So I decide to redirect my energy to what has been advertised as the most difficult ATV trail in the area—twenty-two miles of swampy and mountainous terrain.

I'd only been on the all-terrain vehicle about five minutes before my shoulders felt like they'd been pulled from their sockets. My lower back was so tight I thought it might snap. Still, I pressed on. (For many of us guys, a great and unexplainable pleasure comes from pain like this.)

One of my family members was with me, so I knew that if anything really bad happened, he'd help out. Plus, we were well supplied. The owner of the ATV had packed tow ropes and toilet paper. The latter must have been for the first time you get scared. Well, you know. When you keep passing signs that say things like "Rescue Zone 2A," you know it's going to be an interesting afternoon.

Remarkable vehicles, ATVs. They get into—and back out of—the most absurd places. The only real trouble was when the gears locked following a quick hand-brake at the end of a jarring bridge. I tried to rock the machine back and forth to free the gears when a lady drove by in an ATV the size of Texas. Filling the air once again was that wonderful accent: "Didja lock yu geeah?" Priceless.

Eventually on our way, we passed through water holes and mud runs that sent brown guck over our lower bodies and into our boots. *Yeah!* What is it about boys and dirt? I felt more like John Eldredge giving a *Wild at Heart* demonstration with every new ascent.

1. If you're a leader, you could use a break. Can you sense the benefits of getting out of your standard routine, traveling to a different part of the country,

and going off-roading at breakneck speed? What do you do to reenergize yourself?

Back on the trail, we got our ATVs up to about twenty miles per hour. Coming out of a gulley, I had the urge to goose the throttle and put some distance between the wheels and the ground. I came down on a massive rock, perfectly placed between my wheels, pushing against the metal brush guard, and tilting the nose of the vehicle downward. The rock forced an immediate stop. My chest slammed into the handlebars, and the force of the impact made my hands sting. Having not been fully convinced until that precise moment, I privately acknowledged that I was—and am—an absolute idiot. After I got my breath back, I put the machine into reverse and slowly steered my ATV around the boulder.

After two hours of this nonstop action, I rounded a corner only to be dazzled by one of the most amazing views of rolling mountain terrain I've ever seen. I got off my vehicle, tried to straighten my stiff body, and walked to the edge of a bluff. Accomplishment is a wonderful feeling even when you're exhausted, perhaps especially when you're exhausted. I stood there for a few minutes and thanked God for his beautiful creation.

2. Can you picture yourself standing in awe at the edge of a precipice and almost laughing with delight over what God has made for you to enjoy, even if you got there only after a difficult journey? If you are doing this study with a group, have the members tell about pursuing adventures when

the weariness of leadership had just about defeated them. If you're doing the study alone, record your story here.

Standing with awe at the breathtaking beauty of God's creation was a supernatural experience, and I tried to soak up as much energy and excitement as I could. Standing on that ledge was almost like being in heaven. And then I remembered that I had to ride the ATV back the same way I had come. Like William Wallace battling King Edward in *Braveheart,* I summoned the troops within my soul and marched right back into the jaws of battle. *Freedom!*

As I (Dan) pointed out in chapter 9 of *Leading with a Limp,* weariness is the companion and constant challenge facing every leader. Physical, emotional, mental, and even spiritual exhaustion wage war against leaders. And even when you fight it with everything you've got, you're still in over your head.

3. Respond with a yes or no to the following statements:

   a. *I thrive on chaos.*

   b. *I yearn for downtime, but when I get it, I feel restless.*

   c. *I tend to overcommit my time.*

   d. *My family thinks I'm stressed.*

   e. *People tell me that I'll suffer burnout, but I disagree. I actually feel energized by the constant demands placed upon me.*

   f. *I need to work this hard a little longer because I know relief is just around the corner.*

We don't need to tell you that the demands of leadership are inhuman. No man or woman alive can carry out all the duties of leadership, meet every goal, and keep everything on track. It simply can't be done.

At the same time, being the leader gives us an adrenaline rush that can become addictive. We want to think we can do it all even if every other honest leader we know has told us it's impossible. Leaders push themselves to the limit, and the rationalizations for doing so are plentiful:

- *I'm doing all of this for God.*
- *I'm doing this for my family's future.*
- *I'm trying to make a difference.*
- *If I don't do it, it won't get done.*

Doing Something About Weariness

The first step in dealing with weariness is to acknowledge the truth that we are definitely in over our heads. Although working longer and harder may take us forward, we actually only get closer to the fatigue of the front line, not to the warmth of the rejuvenating fire back in camp.

Furthermore, busyness begets busyness. Fighting to meet deadlines and demands gives us a false energy that makes an impossible challenge even more attractive. The pursuit of the impossible challenge is exhilarating for a short time, but if the pace becomes our new reality, we have lost proper focus and our guiding spirit. It's time to stop, get honest about where we are, and work on actually changing our paradigm.

As soon as the next big deadline looms, the standard rationalizations will fuel more activity and put you right back on the hamster wheel. So when a trusted friend or colleague brings up your weariness and your schedule, resist using the classic defense, "You just don't understand." Instead take the time to talk things out and then figure out an alternative.

4. Consider the last time you pushed hard to meet a deadline. It's crunch time, and the pressure never seems to let up. In the midst of your scrambling, someone mentions that you've been working too many hours and that you really need to pull back. After quelling the urge to physically assault the person, you smile, weakly acknowledge the truth of the statement, and wish that individual could walk in your shoes for a day. Now stop and ask yourself this: why does such a comment make you so angry? One reason could be that you must follow through on what you have committed to do—and there's a lot to get done. But beyond the immediate demands of the current project, why does the suggestion that you need to work fewer hours make you angry?

5. Think beyond the immediate deadline and the current big project. Think about the big picture for a moment as you consider not how to fix the infinite procession of scramble moments but how to avoid them altogether. Clarify your thoughts and ideas as you complete the following statements.

     a. *I am busy because…*

b. *If I could cancel one thing from my regular schedule, it would be…*

c. *My soul feels most rejuvenated when I…*

6. Here's a multiple choice question for you. If you were giving advice to someone who seemed overly stressed due to a crazy work schedule, you would tell that person to:
   a. Start working exactly like I do. Follow my example.
   b. Buck up and make the best of it!
   c. Be sure you are making time for God and your family.
   d. Definitely take time for yourself.
   e. Learn to say no. It's the greatest gift you'll ever give yourself.
   f. Other: _____.

I doubt that you chose option *a* or *b*. And if you didn't, what does that suggest about the advice you should be giving yourself? If, in this hypothetical situation, you chose the helpful advice of options *c* through *e,* do you follow that advice in your own life? Why or why not?

THE TRUTH ABOUT WEARINESS

A limping leader tells the truth: "I struggle like everyone else does, but I've found that if I don't take time to rejuvenate my soul and refuel my body, I will eventually crash and give in to despair." Honestly admitting your brokenness and providing real-life evidence of that brokenness go a long way in leading others. And that same quality—honesty—goes a long way in leading ourselves.

Consider again this wisdom from chapter 9 of *Leading with a Limp:*

> The tipping point that returns us to our First Love is disillusionment about all our lesser loves. What originally led us to serve others by leading them seldom remains our North Star. The sole reason to serve as a Christian is Jesus, yet he is easily lost in the various activities that consume our days. The real cost of busyness, therefore, is the loss of our spiritual vitality. Among the leaders I surveyed, it was a common sentiment that crisis and pressure can energize activity, but they deplete the soul. It costs much in both time and desire to stay connected to spiritual resources—to Jesus—during those times.[1]

7. Would you say that you are truly oriented toward Jesus as your North Star? If not, to what are you oriented? What evidence in your life supports either answer?

8. What would it take to make Jesus your North Star? (Use a big-picture perspective to answer this question.)

9. Are you bold enough to say no more often than yes to opportunities for service and profit? If so, list some specific things you are ready to give up or turn down.

10. Does the organization, church, or ministry that you lead give you the freedom to maintain a healthy balance in your everyday life? Are you given the freedom to set aside time to read, pray, reflect, and weep, if necessary? How about the freedom to play, exercise, and relax? If not, why not? Is it possible that you have not made sure your board or other leaders above you know that these things are essential for you?

Effective leadership reveals itself in the most interesting places. The day following my ATV adventure, I (Matt) had the opportunity to tackle the trail again and maybe go farther this time. My other option was to give in to my daughters' pleas to stay back with them, go swimming, and then maybe go out for ice cream or watch a movie. I chose the latter, and now I see an interesting lesson in all of this.

The night I returned from my ATV ride, I was weary. I put off family requests until another day. I needed some time to rest. By contrast, the night after my relaxing day with my daughters brought laughter, a walk in the woods holding their hands, and a discussion with my older daughter on the issue of forgiveness and getting along with her sister, a conversation that she initiated.

We reap what we sow in our personal lives as well as in our leadership.

Will I go out on the trail again? I'm sure I will. But hopefully I'll do so knowing that I will balance the scales when I return home.

9

◈━━━◈

THREE QUESTIONS
EVERY LEADER MUST ANSWER

In chapter 10 of *Leading with a Limp,* we considered three questions that we all must ask and answer about the practice of limping leadership: *Is it true for me? Is it me? Is it now?* Basically we have to decide if we're ready to embrace a new leadership approach and not just dabble with it on days when we're not pressured to perform. If we choose to embrace the path of broken leadership, we need to know in advance the ways it will change our life as leaders.

Since you're this far in the workbook, we are assuming that you are ready to make significant changes in the way you lead. It's one thing to come up with roles for leaders—roles like mentor, mapmaker, coach, truth-teller, midwife, shepherd, visionary, and so forth. But we need to shift the focus away from what is expected of you as a leader and start asking how you are to lead. The way you answer these "how" questions will largely define how you fulfill your calling as a leader:

- Paul claimed for himself the chief-sinner title. Is this same title a central part of your call as a leader?

- Have you declared this admission of being the chief sinner to those you lead in your organization, church, committee, or ministry team?

- What will you do to live out the calling of a leader who limps?

As you work through this chapter, some sections may seem like the book's conclusion. We actually have a few chapters to go, but for now we're going to give you the opportunity to ask yourself if you really believe that all of this is feasible.

IS IT TRUE FOR ALL LEADERS?

The fact that we have free will means that we are free to mess up. When making choices and decisions, we can contribute to human suffering and even increase our own suffering.

Of course, any leader worth his salt wants the best for his organization. Consequently, some leaders are tempted to reduce suffering through a form of authoritarian order. This is done out of good motives, but the idea that we can reduce suffering in this way is a lie. If you lead in the real world (and who can avoid it?), then you will lead during times when you are broken and in pain. Leaders don't have to choose between being a coach, shepherd, or midwife *and* being broken, foolish, and disillusioned. Instead, our choice is whether or not to be all of these things. Will you be a disillusioned midwife, a foolish shepherd, or a broken coach?

1. As we have seen, the first question of broken leadership is this: *Is it true for me?* Does Paul's confession that he is the chief of sinners mean that each true leader—a person who leads according to the pattern God calls him to—is the most broken person, the biggest failure, the top sinner in the camp? Why or why not?

2. Can you think of a leader you have served who succeeded in meeting goals, increasing profits, and growing the organization, yet failed as a leader? If so, tell that story briefly.

3. When you face frustration as a leader, do you see your broken condition as an advantage or a disadvantage? Explain.

Jesus was the greatest leader in history—indeed, the greatest leader the earth will ever see. And his approach in virtually every area of life was inverted, paradoxical, even mysterious. He added a unique twist to just about every expectation people had about leaders.

4. Think of some of God's inverted expectations, such as childlike faith being the most powerful, the first being the last and the last being first, finding your life by losing it, being blessed when you bless "the least of these," and so forth. God's paradoxical model of leadership is that leaders are first of all servants. Closely related to that is the inverted expectation that leaders are

humble, open, and transparent. Think of an inverted leadership expectation that is especially meaningful to you and explain why it's essential to broken leadership.

5. Give additional thought to the inverted world of a leader who follows God. Is it possible that being a servant who is humble is just the starting point? Does God call you not only to be this type of leader but also to proclaim to those who follow you that you are broken, prone to fail, and, in brief, a fool? Write down your honest reaction to this question.

IS IT TRUE FOR ME?

What do you most desire in your life as a leader? Do you serve in leadership to achieve success in a certain field? Do you enjoy the recognition and visibility that accompany leadership? Did something deeper first convince you to be a leader and now keeps you in that role despite all the reversals? Perhaps the key question is this: What keeps you going? What encourages you to remain in the madness of leadership?

6. Think about the last time you seriously considered resigning from your position as a leader (either paid or volunteer). What prevented you from following through?

Every leader serious about serving God as she leads has asked these questions. The task of leadership is ridiculous. We are required to lead people who largely don't want to be led, or they want the leader to do everything for them. Every year the bar is raised and we're required to produce bigger results than the year before no matter how the economy is doing, what new products and services the competition has introduced, or whether our staffing level has been cut once again. It's no exaggeration to say that it's impossible to lead. No one is equal to the task.

7. The gospel of Jesus offers these radical inversions: strength is found in weakness; where sin is found, grace abounds; the most effective leaders lead with a limp. These are the paradoxical assumptions behind everything we've studied up to this point. Do you believe these things are true? Why or why not? And if you agree they are true, do you believe they are true for you?

IS NOW THE TIME?

You can agree that everyone is broken, even leaders. You can also agree that you are a broken leader. And you can sign on to the idea that if you are to lead in the way God has called you, then you must lead from the position of being your organization's chief sinner.

What is left to every leader is to make these ideas real in the everyday demands, challenges, and wounds of leadership. You may want to lead with all the power, authenticity, and honesty of a limping leader, but then conclude that now is not the time for you to implement any major changes. To start limping now may cost you a job that is crucial for gaining experience necessary for a better position that would put you in a spot to influence many more people with the truth. On the other hand, such reasoning may be nothing more than a smoke screen.

Choosing to lead with a limp is not a decision you can make on your lunch hour. This kind of commitment involves a wholesale change in your orientation, approach, commitments, focus, and daily practices. Discuss the decision with your spouse and a few close friends, seeking their prayers and blessings.

8. In the space that follows, list any questions you still have about limping leadership. List also your doubts, fears, and other hindrances to making this commitment. Ask your spouse or a close confidant to pray with you over these obstacles.

9. Recall a major decision you recently had to make as a leader. What might you have done differently if you were already committed to leading with a limp? Would you have made the same decision in the same way, or would you have arrived at a different decision? Explain your answer.

10. Name the people who serve as your top role models in leadership. In what specific ways do they demonstrate that they are each a broken, flawed mess of a leader?

11. Think about a person who looks to you as a role model. What do you think that person says about you—about your openness, honesty, transparency, and humility—as a leader?

For me (Matt), my role model of limping leadership has always been my dad. An immensely successful businessman, he left his career at its height to go to seminary at the age of fifty. Incredible ministry followed. At age sixty he reentered the business world and enjoyed success once again, but this time he had an entirely new perspective. I asked him what he thought limping leadership might mean. Here's a sample of what he said:

> I would love to be able to tell you that leadership has always been a wonderful experience since I trusted Christ, but that would, of course, be a lie. However, when I have approached true crisis situations with a Christlike demeanor, I have found confidence, resiliency, and the ability to persevere. When I have chosen to approach these situations in my "old man" state, though, I have found false confidence through my use of a heavy hand even while a small voice in my mind was always saying, "I hope no one calls my bluff!"

Will you allow troubling and humbling words to enter your lexicon of leadership? Are you willing to be known as a complete mess, a flawed strategist, a blind guide…a limping leader?

The choice is yours.

10

FORMING CHARACTER, NOT RUNNING AN ORGANIZATION

Limping leaders know that their highest calling is not to lead an organization, not to exceed corporate goals, and not to improve profits, but to grow character. When you analyze your performance as a leader, how do you measure how well you are fulfilling your calling?

If this chapter has one goal, it is to help you think through your daily life as a leader. What factor at your very core exerts the greatest influence in guiding you as a leader?

Let's look at two religious leaders whose stories serve as case studies of leading through character building. They have much to teach us if we'll step back and consider their lives—and our lives in light of theirs. These two leaders hold contrasting beliefs on many topics, but their ability to lead with a limp is the same.

Consider the respective platforms of evangelist Billy Graham and the late Pope John Paul II. Both men have held unequaled positions of influence. Their positions on Christian faith, and their stands and analyses of ethical, political, economic, and diplomatic issues were always reported around the world.

However, the worldwide popularity of these men was not built through media coverage and the public's obsession with celebrity. Instead their popularity grew because of their obvious love of servanthood and their caring for others. Neither man gave in to the temptation to alter his message either to fit current trends or to cater to the preferences of the masses. Both John Paul and Billy Graham chose to use character, both their own and that of Christ, to inspire and lead the world.

Pope John Paul II had strong views on Catholic doctrine and Christian spirituality. He never watered down what he believed, and he could be forceful in response to church disputes. In his book *Crossing the Threshold of Hope,* he wrote: "Indeed, when the true doctrine is unpopular, it is not right to seek easy popularity."[1] But in the public realm, he preferred to keep to the simple things that mattered most. John Paul chose to concentrate publicly on servanthood and the love of Christ.

As part of his legacy, he taught limping leaders this lesson: when you lead with a Christlike character, you have no interest in—and you waste no energy seeking—"easy popularity."

1. Think of a time when you modified a personal belief to gain popularity and fit in more with a social group. Then consider a time when you modified a belief at work to advance an idea or a cause within your own organization. Write both memories below.

2. If the above instance didn't seem to apply to you, consider this one: Does part of you feel that you need to publicize your servanthood instead of simply living it? Do you feel compelled to make sure people are aware of

your recent positive actions? If so, what problems can these motivations cause? Explain.

Leading by Character

In contrast to other leadership styles, leading with a Christlike character makes use of simple messages to transform hearts and change lives. As I (Matt) write this chapter, Billy Graham has just completed what many believe to be his final crusade in the United States, perhaps in the world. He is eighty-six years old, and he suffers from Parkinson's disease. His wife, Ruth, is also ill, and he feels the need to be with her. But he made the sacrifice of being away from her so he could appear in New York City to proclaim his simple message of the redeeming love of Christ to ninety thousand people in a Queens football stadium. His grandson Franklin Graham IV best summed up this man's humility and leadership when he encouraged an audience at the Southern Baptist Convention not to try to emulate the elder Graham: "My grandfather and I would say, 'You're shooting too low.' He'd say, 'Aim higher.' He'd say, 'Just be faithful to the call that you have. God's going to use you.'"[2]

This is no false humility. Franklin Graham, Billy Graham's son, recalled years ago when his father was speaking before ten thousand evangelists. He was asked who would take his place when he retired. He extended his arms to them and said, "You."[3] Anyone who desires to lead with a limp needs to be filled with gratitude for men such as John Paul II and Billy Graham. We, too, through the power of Christ, can have this type of impact in our own circles.

THE MYSTERY OF AWE

The prophet Isaiah was dealing with a universal truth when he said, "Your iniquities have separated you from your God; your sins have hidden his face from you" (Isaiah 59:2). A famous American preacher connected this universal problem of sin with our blindness to the beauty and order of God and his work. Our lack of awe in God's presence and our lack of gratitude for all that God has done and has given us reveals much about our sin and separation from God.

> One has only to consider that frivolous American who in the Rembrandt room of the Amsterdam Gallery looked lackadaisically around and asked: "I wonder if there is anything here worth seeing"; one has only to recall the women who climbed an Alpine height on an autumn day, when the riot of color in the valley sobered into the green of the pines upon the heights, and over all stood the crests of eternal snow, and who inquired in the full sight of all this, "We heard there was a view up here; where is it?" to see that there is a spiritual qualification for every experience, and that without it nothing fine and beautiful can ever be real to any one. "Mr. Turner," a man once said to the artist, "I never see any sunsets like yours." And the artist answered grimly, "No, sir. Don't you wish you could?"[4]

Our souls long for beauty and order, for the awe of God that inspires us with God's glory. With that in mind, answer the following questions:

   3. What is one of your favorite songs or melodies?

4. What aspect of that song or melody makes your heart sing?

5. Do you consider being inspired by this song a supernatural experience? Explain.

6. If you are using this workbook with a group, discuss your answers to questions 3 through 5.

The Bible tells us to "sing to the LORD a new song" (Psalm 149:1). As Dr. Ray Ortlund Jr. taught me, a "new song" does not just mean new in style or sound; it means "redeemed." We are all unique beings, operating in unique settings and paradigms. In each of these situations, we have the opportunity to bring Christ into the process and produce a sense of redemption. Sing this new song for Christ in your own life and then sing that beautiful melody of God into the hearts of those you lead.

BEING A CHARACTER

God calls us to exhibit the character of Christ in our lives—as leaders, as spouses, as friends, as parents. He also calls us to live out our own character as we follow him in all that we do. God wants you to live out who he made you to be.

7. List five people who come to mind when you hear the expression, "He/she is such a character!"

    a.

    b.

    c.

    d.

    e.

8. If you are using this workbook with a group, have each person share a story about one or two of the people on their list of "characters." (We would surmise that most of the names bring positive memories, although negative ones are certainly possible.)

9. Why did the people on your list come to mind? What about them makes them stand out as characters in your life?

The infectious style of some people's character cannot and should not be denied. But you are no less a character with your own idiosyncratic tendencies and traits. If you have not allowed Christ to free you to live out your unique character, though, you may find it difficult to motivate others to follow you with energy and enthusiasm. Faced with that difficulty, most leaders resort to leading from their desire for control instead of their brokenness. Let us explain.

Leadership that is a natural extension of your character means using your flaws and brokenness—as well as your sense of humor and curiosity and compassion and other unique qualities—to lead in honesty and transparency. It's all too common for leaders to do just the opposite. In his book *Under Fire,* Lt. Col. Oliver North had this to say about former Nicaraguan president Daniel Ortega: "It was hard to imagine him as a former guerrilla leader. He reminded me of the joke about the man with 'negative charisma': when this guy enters the room, it feels like three people just left."[5] Ortega had such a negative character that he sucked the life out of any room he entered. Once he arrived, there was less humanity, less life present.

As you consider the need to build positive character in others, consider your own character.

10. Imagine yourself standing in a meeting room. Behind you is a large white-board where you have just taken a black marker (don't you just love that smell?) and written down twenty of your attributes. Some are profound revelations and others are nothing more than favorite activities. Some of the items listed apply directly to your life at work; others to your family life or social life. But each one says something about who you are. Now, in the space below, list twenty of your attributes.

11. Imagine yourself still standing in the meeting room with twenty of your attributes listed on the whiteboard behind you. In front of you sit your colleagues and subordinates. Through open discussion and some of them approaching the board, they create a second list, which is their perception of who you are in each of the same categories. In what ways do you think their list might differ from yours? What might explain any discrepancies between the two lists?

12. If you're really brave, try this exercise at work. Or if you are using this workbook with a group, try the exercise together. More than a few of your attributes are probably perceived quite differently than you would expect. Let these discrepancies serve as a starting point for discussing what it means to lead others as "a real character."

13. Your colleagues and staff know you, but in many ways they don't know you at all. To help them get to know who you really are, look at your list of traits and circle the ones that reveal your brokenness. Usually those are the traits you need to make known as you become a more open and transparent limping leader.

Fear and a desire for control will conspire to prevent you from carrying out this exercise in real life. After all, each of us struggles with the fear of people knowing who we *really* are inside, the unique character that Christ has fashioned, because they may not like us. It's much easier to create a slightly modified version of ourselves—one that is safer, one that casts us in a more complimentary light. We tend to cover our weak points so that we might be seen as strong. We don't realize that nothing takes more strength than leadership that doesn't hide our brokenness.

In chapter 11 of *Leading with a Limp,* we read these words:

> The better a leader tells the stories of grace in his life, the more he invites others to consider their own story and calling. The more he wholeheartedly chooses a life of gospel passion, the more effectively he will call others to goodness. In that sense, a leader either has a character of goodness or not. There are indeed characters whose effect on others is to discourage or derail. They don't live with integrity and authenticity. But a person who lives out his calling to reveal his character invites others to freedom, kindness, and strength.
>
> The church spawns many good-hearted people who don't know their own character.... We are not used to thinking about our character and our role except in terms of what we do. We seldom consider our role in terms of *how* we do what we do.[6]

Drawing on those ideas, consider the following character questions about yourself:
- *Who am I?*
- *Where am I meant to serve?*
- *How am I meant to use my gifts and suffer my weaknesses for good?*

Leaders are storytellers. And limping leaders are in a perfect position to tell a much better story. We are meant to be a community that loves stories about our great need for the gospel, stories celebrating the glory of grace, and stories of how we have come to be who we are. Indeed, our stories of risk are the tales that tell us who we are longing to become.

11

How to Tell a Better Story

In my book *To Be Told,* I (Dan) pointed out that true growth, both in our own lives and in the lives of others, starts with learning to tell our personal stories. This is just as true for leaders as for anyone else. In fact, it could be argued that it is even truer for leaders.

We who lead need to learn how to love the story that God has written for us—both the good parts of our lives and the parts we struggle to accept. As we willingly coauthor the rest of our lives with God, we will be far less fearful of entering into the stories of the people around us. Character and trust are found in the midst of hearing and telling stories—our own as well as the stories of those around us.

In fact, storytellers who develop the art of listening have the ability to transform their organizations into unstoppable entities, organizations that are prepared to reach their full potential. People willingly follow such a leader because she is seen as being real, honest, and accessible.

With his books *In Search of Excellence* and *Thriving on Chaos,* Tom Peters redefined the corporate management style of the 1980s and early 1990s. You would expect others to describe Peters as daring, brilliant, and visionary. However, when asked to endorse one of Peters's books, Paul Weaver of the *Wall Street Journal* described the author as "an enthusiast, a storyteller and a lover of capitalism."[1]

Weaver highlighted three traits you wouldn't expect to find in the same sentence.

Yet Peters was so dedicated to telling his own stories and learning from the stories of other people that storytelling became a part of his identity. The leading financial publication in the free world called him a storyteller.

Storytelling is more important—and more essential to effective leadership—than most of us understand. So if you have chosen to lead with a limp, you must practice the following four steps toward truthful storytelling. Go ahead and move past your fear of self-disclosure and vulnerability. You will gain power as a leader through these practices of storytelling: exploration, dialogue, discernment, and decision.

The First Step: Exploration

Show your team members that you view your relationships with people in the organization as incredibly important. Send out at least five thank-you notes per week. These should be handwritten and addressed by hand. Don't limit the notes to clients and customers. Internal notes are extremely valuable. After your next staff meeting or strategy session, write a note to each participant and let them know how much you appreciate their opinions and expertise. Don't let work get in the way of getting the notes written.

After you master this first step, get more intentional about the exploration stage of storytelling. Choose two or three people from your department or organization who view you as their leader. Invite them out for lunch or coffee sometime in the next week. Let your goal be exploration, not small talk and not problem solving. As you talk over lunch, explore the life of the people sitting at the table. At the same time allow them to explore your life. Let your own dignity and theirs guide you in an honest discussion.

1. During the exploration stage—that time devoted to talking and telling stories over lunch or coffee—listen for areas that you need to revisit later. What issues could affect your department or organization? What was mentioned that you need to follow up on? List those items in the space below.

The Second Step: Dialogue

Candid dialogue is the necessary next step. Dialogue carries exploration into the realm of interpretation. During this stage, the open conversations that characterized the exploration phase will extend to debating various points. Disagreements are sure to arise, and that's part of the purpose. But learn to disagree without insisting on getting the last word. You don't need to be right; you simply need to be a part of the conversation.

So think of ways to enter into dialogue with people on your staff or leadership team. And remember that in pure dialogue you guard yourself against trying to manipulate the content or outcome of the discussion. Everyone is free to express views, and no one is made to feel right or wrong or that there is a penalty for not coming up with the "right answer." Be especially aware of the existence of spin—shading what you say or others obscuring the deeper meaning of what they're saying—including how it could be applied to what they are saying.

2. In chapter 12 of *Leading with a Limp,* this statement is made: "Good dialogue tends to create more chaos and confusion than clarity. It tends to expand the realm of possibilities, both good and ill, that needs to be taken into account."[2] The purpose is not order and simplification but openness and expansion—a broadening of options and an increase in the number of factors to be considered. Do you see the value in such an outcome? If so, what are the primary benefits of dialogue? If not, what are the disadvantages?

The Third Step: Discernment

The next step in learning to tell a better story is discernment, an essential element of leadership that eludes many leaders. Taking the time to explore and then dialogue and even debate does wonders to motivate your staff and enlist their trust and support. However, you're the leader and the buck still stops at your desk.

The purpose of exploration and dialogue is not to shift into leadership by committee. But neither do you want your staff to assume that you will make decisions without taking their input into account. You make the decision; they don't. But you make the decision in light of the stories they have told you during exploration and dialogue.

3. If you have experimented with exploration and dialogue, did you find those steps helpful as you made a major decision for your organization? Explain.

4. If you have not yet tried exploration and dialogue, will you take those two steps before making your next major decision as a leader? Why or why not?

You may be asking: "If the leader is the decision maker, then why waste time with exploration and dialogue? Why not just go ahead and decide and then move on?" The quick answer is that no leader is as smart, insightful, perceptive, or wise as he needs to be. Remember, we lead in the middle of crisis and chaos and complexity. Exploring the terrain by listening to stories from our staff, then dialoguing so that people feel free to disagree, to raise objections, to play devil's advocate—these are needed if a leader is to arrive at the best decision. Storytelling leads to a decision, and the decision will then lead to more storytelling. Remember, a limping leader is called to tell a better story.

5. Write down the mission statement for your organization, church, committee, ministry team, or other group.

6. Answer yes or no to the following questions:
   a. Would you say that the people on your team or in your organization are familiar with this mission statement?
   b. Would you say that the people on your team or in your organization agree wholeheartedly with the mission statement?
   c. If you answered no to question *b,* why do you think there is a lack of support? Summarize the reason(s) below.

If the leader is limping well, the cycle of exploration, dialogue, and discernment will constantly repeat itself. If the team is not prepared to operate from the same page in terms of mission, purpose, and philosophy, discernment will be that much more difficult. But think about this: if part of discernment is taking the time to consider what most honors the unique calling and story of your organization, don't you want to be absolutely sure what that calling and story are?

If your organization's mission statement does not accurately reflect the calling and story of the work you and your team are doing or if the mission statement does not come up in the stories that you tell, then it is either a) inaccurate and ineffective, or b) it has been buried under the bureaucracy that you didn't think you had. In this regard, a limping leader has a clear advantage. He or she uses the limp to make objectives clearer and more attainable.

7. Look again at the preceding comments, then reread your mission statement and think about it. Put it on the agenda for your next staff meeting. At that meeting ask your team members to comment on how closely the mission statement matches the work that your organization actually does. Invite comments about where the discrepancies are most obvious as well as where the inconsistencies are hurting your organization.

It's possible that your mission statement no longer reflects the story that your organization is called to tell. Let the discussion with your staff aid you in discernment as you listen carefully to what is said about both the mission statement and the calling of your organization.

The Fourth Step: Decision

The processes of exploration, dialogue, and discernment have brought you to the decision-making point. No decision is clear or easy. But after you invest effort in properly discerning the situation in light of your mission, goals, staff input, and God's calling, you can make decisions with much more confidence than you've had in the past.

8. Think through your decision-making process and a decision you currently face. What is your greatest anxiety as you prepare to make the decision?

9. Look back at the way you typically prepare to make a decision. Think about all the ways you gather information, consult advisors, study the market, review reports, assess the customer base, analyze trends, and so forth. What is the weakest step in your process? Does it fall into the realm of exploration, dialogue, or discernment? In what way?

10. Once you've made the decision, carefully plan the way you will announce it. Remember that every time you make a decision, someone in your organization will be disappointed or frustrated. So will you be tempted to spin the announcement in an attempt to quiet your critics? In what way? What will you do to guard against spin as you let your staff know the decision that has been made? Consider adding a personal story. It's a good way to avoid spin and remind you of your limitations as a limping leader.

11. If you don't already have a *personal* mission statement, develop one for yourself. As you navigate the waters of discernment on a daily basis, consider the effect of circumstances on your analysis of the present through the objective lens of your mission statement.

12

TELLING SECRETS

In chapter 1 of this workbook, I (Matt) introduced you to Rick, a man who has clearly and effectively led with a limp. Since this chapter focuses on the leader as an organization's chief sinner, it's the perfect place to revisit Rick's life and example. You may recall that in an adult Sunday-school class he'd been leading for eleven years, Rick admitted he had only recently begun to fully believe and experience the truths of God.

Recently I asked Rick to explain the paradox of teaching a Bible class while still grappling with the validity of the Bible's teachings. From time to time, all of us find ourselves not completely accepting biblical principles. But for Rick his spiritual transformation seemed so specific and meaningful. I wondered how it had played out in his life.

Rick said that for many leaders, and certainly for him, it came down to three words: fear, desire, and control. Everything about his life, including his spiritual life, was influenced by one or more of those issues. "It's not that I didn't believe in what God's Word said," he explained. "It's that I didn't believe it was completely true for me."

Rick says his life was governed by questions and statements like these:

- *How might someone expect me to act in this situation? What might people think about me if I don't do what they expect?*

- *I want others to look at me in a certain way, so I need to make it appear as if the desired persona or outcome is true and real. Maybe then I'll even believe it myself.*
- *No one wants to hear about my struggles. If I'm going to lead people, I must control what they are hearing and not hearing.*

Such conflicts rise up from our subconscious and fool us into thinking they represent who we truly are. Rick eventually discovered that he presented himself based on fear, desire, and control. If you desire something strongly enough, the natural next step is to exert as much control as possible to ensure that you get what you want. Eventually you are doing this in every area of life. You become weary of the endeavor, but you can't stop because you fear how others would view you if you were to live in a new way.

Now, it's certainly not uncommon for people to try to control their surroundings even when it comes to spiritual issues. But when we seek to exert control, we are implying that God is smaller than we are, that we can in some way manipulate his actions if we set our antennas the right way and chant a certain magic formula.

Rick's weariness finally met his fear head-on, and at that point a spiritual transformation began. He decided he no longer wanted misplaced desire, control, and fear to dominate his life. He came to understand and embrace the truth that God loved him unequivocally. When he realized he didn't need to prove anything to God, he found he had nothing to prove to anyone else. Rick no longer needed to live in fear that others might find out about the struggles and disbelief that lay just beneath the surface. And then an interesting thing happened. He found that when he decided to be more open about his struggles and fears, he actually became more effective leader.

1. As you consider Rick's story, think about your own story. In what ways do you identify with Rick's experience? In what contexts have you struggled with control, fear, or misplaced desire?

2. Control, fear, and misplaced desire can be negative reasons to speak and act, yet we all succumb to their influence from time to time. List some ways your life has been affected by one or more of these motivators.

WHO NEEDS THE GOSPEL?

It is a great irony that those who proclaim the gospel sometimes need it more than those who hear their proclamation. To not fully understand this, let alone to not accept our need for vast amounts of God's grace, puts a leader on an incendiary life path.

Furthermore, if we have learned that freedom and strength come through admitting our fears and failures, and if we acknowledge that there is indeed a way to tell the truth without sharing all the grimy details, then why don't we tell our people that we are the chief sinner in the organization?

Try these action points:

3. Find a small box with a lid (or make one out of poster board). On a piece of paper, write down your shortcomings, struggles, hidden fears, and failures. When you're done writing, drop these "confessions" into the box. Seal the lid and keep the box in a spot where you will see it every day and be reminded that you are your organization's chief sinner.

4. Think through a "confession of self" story that you would love to tell someone but don't have the guts to share. Sit down at your computer, open a blank document, key in the words of your "confession," read it, and then delete it.

5. List three projects you have started—at home or at work—but then put on the back burner. After each one, note the things that need to happen for you to finish that project. How much time or money, staff or other resources, needs to go toward completion? Also write down whom, if anyone, you should apologize to for not having completed the job—and be sure to apologize.

Living in the Already and Not Yet

In chapter 13 of *Leading with a Limp,* you read about the reality of living in the already and not yet. While our hearts long for the promise of redemption fully realized and experienced, we continue to live on earth, where even redeemed children of God can't avoid failure and sin. We live in the already of God's redemption, but also in the not yet of full freedom from sin and its effects.

The Bible talks about redemption being a past-, present-, and future-tense reality. We *have been* saved. We *are being* saved. One day we *will be* saved. Each of us is a work in progress. We know this, but still we get defensive when our sins are recognized and pointed out by others. We attempt to silence the feedback by offering either excuses or context to mitigate our failure. There were extenuating factors, we were having a bad day, or we were under too much pressure and stress.

Here's the truth: we are redeemed sinners. God has done everything that's necessary to save us, and if we have trusted in the sacrifice of his Son, we are saved. But we are still sinners. We struggle with lust and anger, or what Jesus calls adultery and murder (see Matthew 5:21–28). Leaders who tell the truth must admit their failures. The truth is that Jesus is alive and that our struggles actually highlight how much sin has been covered by God's forgiveness rather than serving as evidence that the Resurrection is not true.

The Tension Between Arrogance and Despair

In chapter 13 of *Leading with a Limp,* you were asked to consider the ramifications of this observation: "What denies the Resurrection in a leader's life is not failure but presumption. Living in the already and not yet gives rise to the tension of living between arrogance and despair."[1]

What does that mean? With regard to arrogance, it means not giving in to presumption by believing you are better than you are. In terms of despair, it means not giving up just because you have failed. As you find the balance between the two extremes, you are living in the tension that honors the Resurrection. With that in mind, answer the following questions pertaining to the tension of living between arrogance and despair.

6. The editors of *Webster's Dictionary* have asked you to write a new definition and more detailed explanation of what it means to live between arrogance and despair. What would you write?

7. Think of someone you work with who tends toward arrogance. Then think of a person who leans more toward despair.

   a. Which person do you resemble the most? In what ways?

b. Ask your spouse or your best friend to tell you whether he or she thinks you most resemble the arrogant or the despairing person. In what ways?

As you think about ways to position yourself between the extremes of despair and arrogance, you will feel the tension between the two. If you struggle with arrogance, consider being more vulnerable when you lead your next staff meeting. Let others know of some ways you are struggling with staffing needs, a drop in revenue, achieving corporate goals, or other organizational issues. Admitting such anxieties helps shift self-reliance to a reliance on God's grace.

On the other hand, if you tend toward despair, you can be more open about that struggle by seeking wisdom and encouragement from your colleagues. Let people know of the despair that sometimes hits you, but also affirm the strength you gain both from God and from being part of a great team. Admitting despair and spreading despair are not the same thing. Don't allow your struggle with despair to infect others. You're a child of God and you're a leader. Believe God's redemption and act on it.

The goal is not to wallow in either extreme—arrogance or despair—but to be open about your struggles and to find balance between the two.

The Tension Between Strength and Tenderness

Just as leaders live in the tension between arrogance and despair, they also need to find the balance between strength and tenderness. First, true strength is the courage to confess cowardice and self-absorption. It is also bold enough to delight in others, to celebrate the mark of glory found in colleagues and staff. A leader's honest gratitude and affirmation encourage people to remain true to their calling. Second, true tenderness steps deeply into the heartache and hopes of others. It suffers and dreams with others without offering cheap piety or an easy way out. A leader's strength must exhibit tenderness, and her tenderness must exhibit strength.

8. Do you lean more naturally toward strength or tenderness? What aspects of your leadership reveal that natural tendency? Be specific.

9. Tenderness can be misunderstood and misapplied as a lack of firmness or the choice to go along with an employee's self-centeredness. But as we've said, true tenderness is tempered with strength. Give an example of how a leader can show tenderness without conceding to the other person's issues.

10. If you are using this workbook with a group, have everyone discuss question 8 (above). As members talk about their natural tendencies, think about the signs of either strength or tenderness you have seen in each person's life.

The Tension Between Wisdom and Innocence

According to the Bible, we are to be "as shrewd as snakes and as innocent as doves" (Matthew 10:16). Our wisdom and cunning must be driven by dovelike innocence, or it will be nothing more than thinly cloaked manipulation. Conversely, a Christian should be harmless but never naive or foolishly innocent.

11. Is it really possible to be crafty and wise yet also be committed to the other person's good? Why or why not?

12. Think of someone you would describe as wise. Does that person also exhibit innocence? If so, describe what that balance between shrewdness and innocence looks like.

Living in this time between the already and the not yet, limping leaders know the tension of paradox. They are both arrogant and despairing, tender yet strong, and wise but innocent. They know the truth of having been redeemed already, of being redeemed today, and of looking forward to the future day when they will be fully redeemed.

Limping leaders embrace the inverted reality of God's kingdom. In that realm where strength comes through weakness, it's not a big stretch to accept that we should be both serpents and doves. Broken leaders learn to balance seeming opposites.

13

$\Longleftrightarrow\!=\!\Longrightarrow$

PROPHET, PRIEST, AND KING: THE THREE OFFICES OF LEADERSHIP

Jesus Christ, the embodiment of all that was good and pure, lived his life for us as the perfect Prophet, the loving Priest, and the eternal King. These were his signatures, and by them he changed the world forever.

Because we are created in the image of God, each of us bears a certain measure of these secret signatures. We, too, serve as prophets, priests, and kings when we serve others. The question is not whether we are called to fulfill these offices—we are. The challenge is to discover the one office with which we most identify and then to seek out and embrace other leaders and colleagues who fill the offices where we most lack.

PROPHET, PRIEST, OR KING?

In every chapter of this workbook, you have been asked to respond to questions and to think through problems. Without realizing it you were revealing areas in which you function as prophet, priest, or king. Although it is not uncommon for people to have abilities in more than one area, it is also very likely that the composite of your answers would reveal your predominant trait.

Let's review the distinctives of these three offices, summarized here from chapter 14 of *Leading with a Limp:*

- *King:* creates and builds infrastructure to provide for the needs of his people, juggles crises, makes decisions, allocates resources, develops talent
- *Priest:* delivers the law, acts according to the king's wishes, creates stories, institutes symbols and narrates others through life, translating when necessary
- *Prophet:* creates compelling vision and awakens desire, disrupts the paradigm of comfort and complacency

As we interact with other leaders, with our colleagues, and with staff members, we need to recognize our own predominant gift as well as the giftings of those we work with. We will attain success only to the degree that we give each office the freedom and scope necessary to operate effectively:

- *Kings* must have the freedom and power to create policies, procedures, and standards of performance; to determine compensation based on performance; to hire, fire, advance or demote employees; and to develop and retain talent.
- *Priests* must have the freedom to create mission, vision, and values that are centered on meaning, stories, and branding in order to foster connection, care, forgiveness, honor, and growth.
- *Prophets* must have the freedom to create new ways of thinking through encounters with truth—encounters that provoke disequilibrium, desperation, and suffering, yet lead to mystery, paradox, desire, and dreams.
    1. Think about your approach to leadership in light of these three offices, then rank the offices, starting with the one you most closely identify with.

        a.

        b.

        c.

I (Dan) am predominantly a prophet who has fair abilities as a priest and poor tendencies as a king. I (Matt) am a good king, an average priest, and a poor prophet. Prophets and kings don't naturally mix, so why are the two of us such a good team? I suppose it's due to the commonality of our second trait as priest.

But we believe it goes much deeper than that. A mutual respect guides us, along with our willingness to admit our failings and an ability to delight in the other's strengths. We try to remember that part of our goal as leaders is to not only lead people but also to serve them. When leaders of different giftedness respect one another, a synergy and a creativity result that far exceed what can be found in only one perspective. C. S. Lewis wrote about the secret signature—the distinguishing trait—in a person's soul. Do we have the ability, or more important, the willingness, to admire this secret signature in ourselves and in others, and to recognize that it radiates the presence of Christ in each of us?

2. Next to each of the three leadership offices, list as many people as you can think of—in your organization, your church, and your family—that have this office as their predominant gift:

   a. king

   b. priest

   c. prophet

3. For which of the three categories did you list the greatest number of people? Were you surprised to see that? Why or why not?

4. Is that category the same as your own predominant trait or a different one? Why is this similarity or difference significant?

5. Are you protective of the tasks and functions associated with the gifting that comes most naturally to you? As you look at the names of people who have the same leadership gift as you, are you threatened by them? Do you feel competitive toward them? If you sense you're being territorial and protecting your turf or your area of influence, what do you think is behind that feeling?

6. Are there many prophets on your sheet? Are you also a prophet? Do you tend to shy away from prophets? Why do you think that's the case?

7. Toward which role do you most wish you had more of a personal inclination? Have you surrounded yourself with others who bear this trait?

8. Do you see the value of having each role represented in an organization, or does this approach threaten your ideas about how to lead effectively? Explain.

Limping leaders realize that to succeed in leadership they must put all three types of leaders in a room and ask them each to value the strengths of the others more than they value their own. An organization needs all three leaders—prophet, priest, and king—to thrive. An imbalance of one or two, without all three, will serve the organization poorly.

Left alone, the king will become a dictator who hates chaos. The priest, if operating without the other two typeset of leaders, will fall into accommodation to avoid conflict. A prophet, if left alone, will indulge in drama and self-absorption to escape boredom. The three need one another, but the initial tension of having to work together—to lead together—will inevitably be greater than the immediate benefits. Over time, however, the three working together will provide leadership unequaled by any individual leader working alone.

To be an effective prophet, priest, or king requires, among other qualities, the knowledge that we are simply one part of the whole. Look again at question 2 and the names on your three lists, especially the names of people whose predominant leadership trait is different from yours. You need these people. Embrace them, learn from them, and lead them—or lead with them—so that each of you is bringing the best of who you are to the call of serving others.

And as you fulfill your calling as prophet, priest, or king, remember that the greatest leaders in Scripture were flawed, reluctant, broken, and sinful. They all led with a definite limp. Thomas à Kempis, the renowned theologian from the fifteenth century, wrote these words:

> Why will you prefer yourself before another, since there are many more learned and more skillful in the law than you are? If you will know or learn anything profitably, desire to be unknown and to be esteemed as nothing.... It is great wisdom and high perfection to esteem nothing of ourselves and to think always well and highly of others.... All of us are frail, but you ought not to think anyone more frail than yourself.[1]

It becomes much more difficult to think you're more important than others in your organization when you come to terms with your identity as the chief sinner in your company, your church, your ministry, your project team, your family. Remember Paul's words: "Christ Jesus came into the world to save sinners, of whom I am chief" (1 Timothy 1:15, NKJV).

To increase your effectiveness as a leader and your impact for the gospel, you must choose to believe that it is possible to gain a more controlled purpose by giving up your desire for control; to gain the trust of others by being more open and vulnerable; and to accentuate the strength of your talents by embracing the opposite talents in others. It is a high calling but one that bears far greater dividends than you will ever know in this lifetime.

So be bold. Go ahead and lead. And don't worry about that limp.

Notes

Introduction
1. Robert K. Greenleaf, *The Power of Servant Leadership* (Mahwah, NJ: Paulist, 1977), quoted in Rueben P. Job and Norman Shawchuck, *A Guide to Prayer for Ministers and Other Servants* (Nashville: Upper Room, 1983), 61.

Chapter 1
1. G. K. Chesterton quote found at www.quotationspage.com/quotes/ G._K._Chesterton (accessed on October 12, 2005).

Chapter 2
1. Alan Downs, *The Fearless Executive: Finding the Courage to Trust Your Talents and Be the Leader You Are Meant to Be* (New York: AMACOM, 2000), 12.
2. David Baron, *Moses on Management: 50 Leadership Lessons from the Greatest Manager of All Time* (New York: Pocket Books/Simon & Schuster, 1999), 170, emphasis added.
3. Baron, *Moses,* 171–172.

Chapter 3
1. Dan B. Allender, PhD, *Leading with a Limp* (Colorado Springs, CO: Water-Brook, 2006), 50–51.

Chapter 4
1. Lyrics by Kathy Troccoli, © Copyright 2000 Sony/ATV Songs LLC/BMI. All rights reserved. Used by permission.

2. Carlo Carretto, *The God Who Comes* (Maryknoll, NY: Orbis, 1974), 183.

3. Allender, *Leading*, 73.

Chapter 8

1. Allender, *Leading*, 130.

Chapter 10

1. Pope John Paul II, *Crossing the Threshold of Hope* (New York: Knopf, 1994), 173.

2. Michael Foust, "Southern Baptists Focus on Evangelism at SBC" (Baptist Press, July 2, 2005), reported online at www.bcnm.com/ministries/communication/07022005/two.htm (accessed on October 12, 2005).

3. Rachel Zoll, "The Next Billy Graham? Religion Experts Say There Won't Be One" (The Associated Press, June 27, 2005), reported online at www.rickross.com/reference/tv_preachers/tv_preachers30.html (accessed on October 12, 2005).

4. Harry Emerson Fosdick, *The Meaning of Prayer* (Nashville: Abingdon, 2003), 88.

5. Oliver L. North with William Novak, *Under Fire: An American Story* (New York: HarperCollins, 1991), 230.

6. Allender, *Leading*, 153–4.

Chapter 11

1. Paul Weaver, quoted in the endorsements for Tom Peters, *Thriving on Chaos: Handbook for a Management Revolution* (New York: Harper & Row, 1987).

2. Allender, *Leading*, 167.

Chapter 12

1. Allender, *Leading*, 168.

Chapter 13

1. Thomas à Kempis, *Of the Imitation of Christ* (New Kensington, PA: Whitaker, 1981), 14.

Where has your leadership journey taken you? Up the
corporate ladder? Into the wilderness? On a lonely vigil?
Into your deepest self? To your knees?

the **LEADERSHIP CRUCIBLE**

Journey with us to a different place.
Experience leadership in a whole new way.
MHGSCONFERENCES.COM

To learn more about WaterBrook Press and view
our catalog of products, log on to our Web site:
www.waterbrookpress.com

WATERBROOK
PRESS